P9-DGM-477

LiVE iT!

Building Skills for Christian Living

My Family

Abingdon Press
Nashville

Live It!
Building Skills for Christian Living

My Family

Copyright © 2005 by Abingdon Press
All rights reserved

No part of this work may be reproduced or transmitted in any form or by any means, electronic or mechanical, including photocopying and recording, or by any information storage or retrieval system, except as may be expressly permitted by the 1976 Copyright Act or by permission in writing from the publisher with the exception of pages displaying the following notice:

© 2005 Abingdon Press. Permission is granted for the original purchaser to reproduce this page for use in the local church or educational setting. Copyright notices must be included on reproductions.

Requests for permission should be submitted in writing to Abingdon Press, 201 Eighth Avenue South, P.O. Box 801, Nashville, Tennessee, 37203; faxed to 615-749-6128; or sent via e-mail to permissions@abingdonpress.com.

Scripture quotations in this publication, unless otherwise noted, are from the New Revised Standard Version of the Bible, copyright © 1989 by the Division of Christian Education of the National Council of the Churches of Christ in the United States of America, and are used by permission. All rights reserved.

Scripture quotations marked (CEV) are from the Contemporary English Version, © 1991, 1992, 1995 by American Bible Society. Used by permission.

Scripture quotations noted NIV are taken from the HOLY BIBLE, NEW INTERNATIONAL VERSION, Copyright © 1973, 1978, 1984 by International Bible Society. Used by permission of Zondervan Publishing House. All rights reserved.

If you have questions or comments, call Curric-U-Phone, 800-251-8591, a toll-free service available Monday through Friday from 8:00 to 4:00 Central Time. Calls at other times are recorded for response the next working day. Or e-mail Curric-U-Phone at curricuphone@cokesbury.com any time.

Editor: Marcia J. Stoner
Production Editor: Melanie Munnell
Design: Randall Butler
Cover Design: Roy Wallace III
Cover Photo: Getty Images USA Inc.

ISBN 0-687-06246-2

05 06 07 08 09 10 11 12 13 14 — 10 9 8 7 6 5 4 3 2 1

Manufactured in the United States of America

CONTENTS

About the Writers

James H. Ritchie, Jr., Ed.D. lives in Monroeville, Pennsylvania, where he writes curriculum, teaches, and serves as a consultant with Ritchie Faith Span Ministries. He developed the *Created By God* sexuality education resources, which are published by Abingdon Press.

Robert St. John lives in LaVergne, Tennessee. Robert currently works for the State of Tennessee as an alcohol and drug addiction specialist. In his spare time Robert has taught sixth grade Sunday school classes and written Sunday school curriculum for preteens.

HOW TO USE THIS BOOK

Live It! is a series of short-term studies that begin with the life issues facing tweens and use the Bible to help tweens develop skills that will help them live as disciples of Christ today and throughout their lives.

Live It! can be used with tweens in a variety of settings. It is designed to be used with fifth- and sixth-grade students, with optional use up to seventh grade.

Live It! Settings

- Sunday school
- Wednesday nights
- Short-term studies coinciding with other short-term church events

Parental Involvement

There is an article on page 62 for parents. Please reproduce this article and send it home to parents so that they will know what their tweens are learning.

Each book of the *Live It!* series has six sessions for tweens and an optional "Tweens and Parents Together" session where tweens and parents can come together and develop better communication skills. This joint session can be done as part of your regular session time and setting, or you can have this session at a time when it can be expanded and an event like a meal can be part of the experience.

You might wish to do a parenting class that corresponds to the same time frame as your tween sessions for the parents of your tweens. The parenting class could meet jointly with your tween class for the seventh session.

Faith Friends

It is very important to begin developing faith mentors/models for your tweens. This is a model for the very beginnings of a mentoring relationship. See page 63 for specifics on how to set up a Faith Friends program.

Inserted into this book are Faith Friends Emergency Cards. These are for your tweens to have with contact information for their Faith Friends and also for Faith Friends to have contact information for the tweens they have agreed to mentor.

THE POINT

Our faith makes a difference in the differences we make in our unique and imperfect families.

THE SKILLS

Tweens will
• understand their place in their family.
• discover what it means to live in a family as people of faith.

THE BIBLE

Genesis 16:1-6; Deuteronomy 6:1-9; 2 Timothy 1:5-7

THE PLAN

PREPARE yourself

Family is not an easy place to be. Making the best of being a tween is complicated when families become a significant source of conflict rather than a support in the midst of it.

The Victorian ideal of the "Christian family" probably generated more guilt in families than healing or comfort, assuming that families were to structure themselves and behave like little churches, complete with in-home opportunities for worship and education. The flaw in that assumption? Churches, unlike

PREPARE your session

Stuff to collect:
- [ ] NRSV Bibles
- [ ] nametags
- [ ] markers
- [ ] construction paper
- [ ] tape
- [ ] glue
- [ ] scissors
- [ ] pencils and pens
- [ ] packages of index cards
- [ ] small boxes of paper clips
- [ ] masking tape or pushpins
- [ ] large sheets of paper
- [ ] **"Affirmation of Us" poster, p. 64**
- [ ] **Faith Friends Emergency Cards**
- [ ] **Faith Friends Program Information, p. 63**
- [ ] **Reproducible 1A, p. 11**
- [ ] **Reproducible 1B, p. 12**

For ☼ *cool options*:
- [ ] multicolored plastic-coated wire (can be found in local craft stores), plastic foam (any thickness will do), chenille sticks, clay

Stuff to do:
1. Make photocopies of Reproducibles 1A and 1B.

For ☼ *cool options*:
2. Using a serrated knife, cut the plastic foam into blocks, approximately 3 inches by 6 inches (see "The Shape of My Family" activity).

families, are voluntary organizations. Once persons reach the teen or young-adult years, they volunteer to be part of the church because they want to behave like a church behaves. Families are formed by other forces and tend to behave like families. Family behavior often falls short of the Victorian ideals that fail to recognize and affirm the diversity that is part of family life.

Tweens are discovering that they are different and doing so at a time when they would prefer to be like everyone else. This means that they want their families to be like everyone else's family—even if no family measures up to the mental image of what they think family should be.

Biblical families do inform us as to the complicated emotions surrounding families. However, Bible families offer poor role models, often falling even further short of the Victorian ideals than our own families do. The solution? Rather than looking to families as the models for how we are to live as the church, or to churches as models for how we are to live as families, we take our families to church and there receive the graces and learn the skills for living as faithful disciples of Jesus in the world and in our families.

GATHER

Welcome and Tag Them Time: 5 minutes

Have tweens write their names on nametags (or index cards using tape to make them into nametags). Beneath their names they are to write a word or phrase describing their role in their family.

The Shape of My Family Time: 10-15 minutes

Ask each tween to cut from a piece of construction paper one geometric shape (circle, square, triangle, or rectangle) for each member of their family, including themselves. Have them glue the pieces to another piece of construction paper and then label each shape with the name of the person in their family that it represents. Remind them that pets are often considered to be family members, as are persons they relate to like brothers and sisters, parents and grandparents, aunts, uncles, and cousins.

Have tweens talk about their family creations. When each person comes to the figure representing himself or herself, point out the word(s) on their nametags describing their role in the family.

Teacher Tip: "Gather" activities are designed to help tweens begin to define their roles in their own families and to help them understand that not all families are the same, but God can be at work in any kind of family.

Stuff–Welcome and Tag Them:

❏ nametags (or index cards and tape)

❏ markers

Stuff–The Shape of My Family:

❏ construction paper

❏ scissors

❏ glue

❏ pens or markers

❏ *cool options:* plastic foam, wire, pencils, chenille sticks, clay

Cool Option: Create a wire sculpture to represent each family member, leaving some extra wire on each figure so that it can be inserted in a piece of plastic foam for mounting. Use pencils to wrap the wire around in order to make spirals and small circles.

Cool Option: Create sculptures from chenille sticks or clay.

INTERACT

Build Three-Dimensional Family To-Do Lists
Time: 10-15 minutes

Help your tweens understand how different families function. Divide participants into smaller groups of unequal sizes—two, three, four, or five persons. If your class is smaller than five, let them work as a single group. If it is larger than fourteen, you may have to repeat the size of some groups.

Once the groups are established, give each group a package of index cards, a box of paper clips, and one marker per person.

Say: Your task is to work together in your small groups—which we are now going to call families—to create a three-dimensional family "to-do" list. Write on the index cards things that families do—one per card—then create a free-standing, three-dimensional "to-do" list using only the cards on which you have written and the paper clips.

Choose at least five (but not all) of the criteria in the box on page 8 by which you will judge each family's creation *but do not share the criteria with the participants until after they are done*. Pick at least one or two criteria that would be difficult or impossible to do or that have nothing to do with the task assigned. (The point of the activity is that in families we often have to work without a "plan" for building a family and by a set of criteria we don't know or understand.)

Call time and report the criteria for judging the creations with the explanation that these criteria are what make for the most ideal construction of a three-dimensional "to-do" list. Expect criticism of your timing ("*Now* you tell us!") and of your choice of criteria ("That's impossible"). Rank each family's creation, rating each criterion on a scale of one to five (five being the highest). Add up the ratings and announce the winner (if any have scored).

Invite tweens to air their feelings about the activity—the project itself, the process of judging, the criteria for ranking and where they came from, and not knowing what was expected of the families

Stuff–Build Three-Dimensional Family To-Do Lists:

❑ packages of index cards

❑ small boxes of paper clips

❑ markers

Teacher Tip: Tweens really get in to this kind of activity, since many of them are physical learners who enjoy manipulating materials. The downside is that they really get in to this kind of activity, and will spend an entire session on it if not encouraged to move along.

ahead of time. **Say: Some people feel as though this happens to their families—imposing criteria for what makes a functional family after the family is already functioning.**

Ask: Name one behavior you have exhibited during the past two activities that you consider to be typical for how you interact with your real family. Give them each time to respond by completing this sentence, "In my family I tend to be the one who…" Compare this response to what they have written on their nametags.

CRITERIA

CRITERIA	RANKINGS							
	Family A	Family B	Family C	Family D	Family E	Family F	Family G	Family H
1. reached the ceiling								
2. used all of the cards originally distributed								
3. has an hourglass shape								
4. covers at least four square feet of table/ floor space								
5. used the most interlocking paper clips								
6. family prayed together before starting construction								
7. assembled the fastest								
8. family that worked together without any conflict								
9. "to do" list most closely matches that of a traditional family								
10. family worked in complete silence								
TOTALS								

Stuff—One Bible Family:

☐ **Reproducible 1A, p. 11**

☐ pens or pencils

Answer for Reproducible 1A:

1. Women who could not have children were believed to be cursed by God.
2. Having slaves was permissible.
3. Having more than one wife was OK.
4. Hagar was proud and hateful toward Sarai.
5. Sarai blamed Abram even though the whole thing was her idea.
6. Abram tells Sarai she can treat Hagar however she wants.
7. Sarai began treating Hagar harshly.

One Bible Family: What's Wrong With This Picture? Time: 10-15 minutes

Say: Some people think that the Bible has family role models to offer us. What it contains is stories about real families, not exemplary families. Let's look at one.

Pass out photocopies of the reproducible "One Bible Family" (**Reproducible 1A, p. 11**). Read the story together and then have the tweens list what they see is wrong. Discuss their responses together.

Say: This is not what we consider to be a good or a typical family today, but it was a family. The amazing thing was God's ability to take this particular family, with all of its real problems, and begin shaping a people of faith.

A Faith Guide for Family Life Time: 5-10 minutes

Pass out photocopies of **Reproducible 1B, p. 12**.

Say: The Bible has some things to say about family life, but it has lots more to say about living as people of faith—things we can apply to how we live in our families. God's people in Bible times and today find Deuteronomy 6:4-9 to be particularly helpful. Can you follow the numbered clues and complete the passage?

Have the tweens complete the puzzle at the top of **Reproducible 1B**. When they are finished, have them do the Reality Check at the bottom of the page, based in part on those verses. Discuss what families could do to spiritually strengthen the family.

Read together 2 Timothy 1:5-7. Remind your tweens that this is a way that family plays an important part in developing their spiritual lives.

DEPART Time: 2 minutes

Mount the "Affirmation of Us" poster on the wall and together repeat the "Affirmation of Us."

Pray: God who listens to us when our families make us crazy, who is present with us when our families rescue us from craziness: Thank you for making a difference in our lives and helping us to make a difference in our families. Amen.

PLAN PLUS

TV Families Time: 10 minutes

Extra time? Ask tweens to create a list of five TV families. Make a chart listing the families (see example below). At the top of column #1, list one characteristic of the first family, and then add a check in the box beside each family if they also evidence that characteristic. Continue until you have listed two or three characteristics for each family, and then add up each column.

Family	Characteristics		
	#1	#2	#3

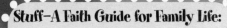
Stuff–A Faith Guide for Family Life:

❏ NRSV Bibles

❏ **Reproducible 1B, p. 12**

❏ pens or pencils

Answer for Reproducible 1B:

Hear, O Israel: The Lord is our God, the Lord <u>alone</u>. You shall <u>love</u> the Lord your God with all your <u>heart</u>, and with all your <u>soul</u>, and with all your <u>might</u>. Keep these <u>words</u> that I am commanding you <u>today</u> in your <u>heart</u>. Recite them to your <u>children</u> and talk about them when you are at <u>home</u> and when you are <u>away</u>, when you lie <u>down</u> and when you <u>rise</u>. Bind them as a sign on your <u>hand</u>, fix them as an emblem on your <u>forehead</u>, and write them on the doorposts of your house and on your <u>gates</u>.

Stuff–Depart:

❏ **"Affirmation of Us" poster, p. 64**

❏ masking tape or pushpins

Stuff–TV Families:

❏ large sheets of paper

❏ markers

Ask: Do those characteristics that were found the most often describe what it means for a group of people to be a family? Are there any on the list that do not describe all families? Are there characteristics that are missing, ones that should be common to all families? How would Abraham and Sarah's family fit into this chart? How would your families fit into the chart?

Family Just Wouldn't Be Family Without...
Time: 5-10 minutes

Stand in a circle. Check your pulse on your wrist or neck. Using that as your rhythm, start the group moving to the left with that rhythm—step, together, step, together. Once the beat has been established, start this refrain:

I say from experience, say without doubt, families just wouldn't be families without...

As the tweens continue to move, go to a large sheet of paper you have mounted on the wall, and invite them to complete that sentence with those things that make families, families. Record their responses and then start the refrain again. After each repetition, have them offer more things to add to the list. Direct them back to the index cards from the "Build Three-Dimensional Family To Do Lists" activity for some ideas. Ask them to look at the completed list, and each select what they consider to be the top three qualities that families should evidence in order to be families. Tally the responses to see what the group considers to be the top three qualities.

Faith Friends

If you are going to have a Faith Friends program, remove and separate the Faith Friends Emergency Cards. Refer to p. 63 for more information on the Faith Friends program.

Stuff–Family Just Wouldn't Be Family Without...:

❑ large sheet of paper

❑ marker

❑ index cards from "Build Three-Dimensional Family To-Do Lists" activity

Stuff–Faith Friends:

❑ **Faith Friends Emergency Cards**

❑ **Faith Friends Program Information, p. 63**

One Bible Family:
What's Wrong With This Picture?

To a family in the time of Abram, children were very important. A woman who did not have a child was looked down upon, and it was children who carried your name into the future.

Abram (Abraham) had been chosen by God to lead God's people. He was promised to be the father of many generations. Abram and his wife, Sarai (Sarah), were old, and after years of waiting for God's promise to be fulfilled they were still waiting for a child of their own. Sarai lost patience.

Read the following story and then list seven things that seem wrong—from our perspective as twenty-first century Christians.

Abram's wife Sarai had not been able to have any children. But she owned a young Egyptian slave woman named Hagar, and Sarai said to Abram, "The LORD has not given me any children. Sleep with my slave, and if she has a child, it will be mine." Abram agreed, and Sarai gave him Hagar to be his wife. This happened after Abram had lived in the land of Canaan for ten years. Later, when Hagar knew she was going to have a baby, she became proud and was hateful to Sarai.

Then Sarai said to Abram, "It's all your fault! I gave you my slave woman, but she has been hateful to me ever since she found out she was pregnant. You have done me wrong, and you will have to answer to the LORD for this." Abram said, "All right! She's your slave, and you can do whatever you want with her." But Sarai began treating Hagar so harshly that she finally ran away.

(Genesis 16:1-6, CEV)

1. _____

2. _____

3. _____

4. _____

5. _____

6. _____

7. _____

© 2005 Abingdon Press. Permission is granted for the original purchaser to reproduce this page for use in the local church or educational setting. Copyright notice must be included on all reproductions.

A Faith Guide for Family Life

Use the numbered definitions below to discover the correct word to fill in the blanks. Compare your results with Deuteronomy 6:4-9.

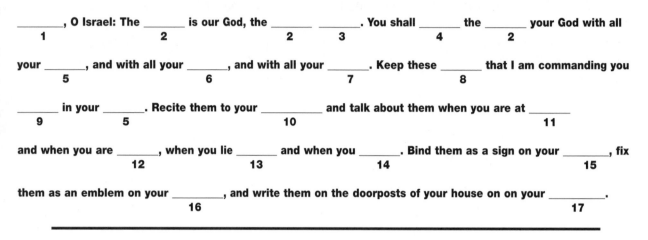

_____, O Israel: The _____ is our God, the _____ _____ . You shall _____ the _____ your God with all
   1   2   2   3   4   2

your _____, and with all your _____, and with all your _____. Keep these _____ that I am commanding you
       5   6   7   8

_____ in your _____. Recite them to your _____ and talk about them when you are at _____
   9   5   10   11

and when you are _____, when you lie _____ and when you _____. Bind them as a sign on your _____, fix
                  12   13   14   15

them as an emblem on your _____, and write them on the doorposts of your house on on your _____.
                          16   17

---

1. another word for listen **2.** another name for God **3.** not together **4.** more than like **5.** blood pump
6. the part of you that connects to God **7.** power, strength **8.** what it takes to make sentences
9. not yesterday or tomorrow **10.** sons and daughters **11.** be it ever so humble, there's no place like it
12. this is where I'm going and I'm never coming back **13.** not up **14.** not fall **15.** human forepaws
16. between scalp line and eyebrows **17.** the portions of fences that swing open

Reality Check	Already doing it	Tried it, didn't work	Haven't tried it yet but we could	Haven't tried it and doubt that it would work
1. Worshiping together on a regular basis.				
2. Talking together about God comfortably as a family.				
3. Testing family decisions by how well they demonstrate love for God.				
4. Praying together at home at meal times.				
5. Serving God together by reaching out to others.				
6. Having prayer partners.				
7. Calling a time out for prayer at times of family conflict.				
8. Displaying symbols at home to remind family members of their shared faith.				
9. Giving family members space to have different understandings of faith.				

© 2005 Abingdon Press. Permission is granted for the original purchaser to reproduce this page for use in the local church or educational setting. Copyright notice must be included on all reproductions.

PARENTING AND KIDDING

THE POINT

Our faith gives us tools for understanding and relating to the persons who parent us.

THE SKILLS

Tweens will
- better understand the role of parenting.
- learn cooperation.
- discuss timing and communication.

THE BIBLE

Ephesians 6:1-4; Deuteronomy 21:18-21; Luke 15:11-32

THE PLAN

PREPARE yourself

If parents are responsible for *parenting*, aren't kids responsible for *kidding*?

Tweens suggesting that their parents have lost their minds is hardly novel. However, the mental images playing in their heads as they say it could actually express exasperation as they labor to bridge the broad divide between parent and tween understandings of what is reasonable or sane. When feeling powerless, as when emotions are running out of control and bodies are right behind, taking potshots at parents is understandable. Tweens who ask their parents, "Are you nuts?" could very well be praying for an answer such as, "No, and while you might feel as though you are, you aren't."

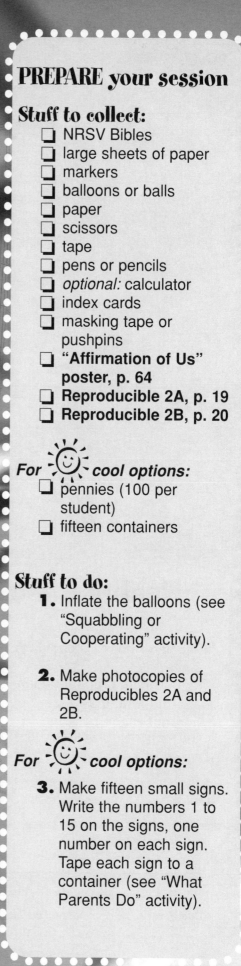

PREPARE your session

Stuff to collect:
- ❑ NRSV Bibles
- ❑ large sheets of paper
- ❑ markers
- ❑ balloons or balls
- ❑ paper
- ❑ scissors
- ❑ tape
- ❑ pens or pencils
- ❑ *optional:* calculator
- ❑ index cards
- ❑ masking tape or pushpins
- ❑ **"Affirmation of Us" poster, p. 64**
- ❑ **Reproducible 2A, p. 19**
- ❑ **Reproducible 2B, p. 20**

For ☼ cool options:
- ❑ pennies (100 per student)
- ❑ fifteen containers

Stuff to do:
1. Inflate the balloons (see "Squabbling or Cooperating" activity).

2. Make photocopies of Reproducibles 2A and 2B.

For ☼ cool options:
3. Make fifteen small signs. Write the numbers 1 to 15 on the signs, one number on each sign. Tape each sign to a container (see "What Parents Do" activity).

In the story of the prodigal son (**Luke 15:11-32**), is it sane for a father to comply with his younger son's demand to get his inheritance "pre-mortem" and to leave home? Of course not! And it would have been even more insane in the ears of Jesus' listeners. His original hearers knew full well that this father was being too unconventional to be believed. His response of radical love had no parallel in their culture or faith. Today, parents throw up their hands and say, "I don't know what to do! I don't want to risk alienating him!" Back then, their course was set. According to Deuteronomic directives, stubborn, rebellious, gluttonous, drunken sons were subject to public stoning (**Deuteronomy 21:18-21**).

Jesus wanted his followers to visualize a new image of the relationship between parent and child. Jesus' point might have been, "Look at how a faith-driven parent deals in a loving, God-like fashion with children struggling—often in less than appropriate ways—to discover who they are."

GATHER

Wall of Words   Time: 5 minutes

Post two large sheets of paper on a wall. Greet tweens as they arrive and ask them to write or illustrate on one sheet things their parents do that drive them crazy or make them angry. On the other sheet ask them to write or illustrate things that they do that they think may drive their parents crazy or make their parents angry.

Squabbling or Cooperating   Time: 7 minutes

Part I: Have the tweens form a circle. Call out one of the things from the parents paper in the "Wall of Words" and throw the balloon to somebody in the circle. The person to whom you threw the balloon will call out something from the tweens paper. Continue in this fashion, until all have had the balloon. Repeat throwing in the same order. After you have done it twice through, start a second balloon after the first, following the same order— and then a third. If there isn't enough confusion, add more.

Part II: Give each person a balloon. Instruct the tweens to see if they can keep their balloons off the ground for thirty seconds— each person on his or her own. Next, have each tween who is right-handed use the right hand to grab his or her left ankle behind his or her back; have each tween who is left-handed use the left hand and right ankle to do the same thing—then once

Stuff–Wall of Words:

- ❏ two large sheets of paper

- ❏ markers

Stuff–Squabbling or Cooperating:

- ❏ balloons (one for each student; may substitute balls)

again each person should try to keep his or her own balloon in the air for thirty seconds. The next step will be for each tween to toss a balloon in the air and then quickly reach behind his or her back and grasp one arm with the other hand—then try to keep the balloon aloft for thirty seconds. Finally, have them work together to keep all of the balloons in the air for a full minute, hands behind backs and hopping on one foot.

Ask: How did our success rate as a group change when we cooperated to keep all of the balloons in the air? Will people cooperate when they are busy being angry?

Bottom Skootch   Time: 5-10 minutes

Have tweens form a circle as large as space allows and sit on the floor. Have them number off by twos. Have the tweens use paper to cut out large *P*s for the *ones* and *K*s for the *twos* and have them tape them on their fronts. **Say: Ones, you are the parents. For this activity, we need you to try to think like a parent. Twos, you are the preteens. Just think like yourselves. The object is for the parents and preteens to come together in the center. I'll be reading several situations. If the parents think this is something where parents would be drawn closer to their kids, they are to move one bottom skootch toward the center of the circle. If it is something where parents and kids would be pushed apart, they are to move one skootch toward the outside of the circle. The kids are to do the same—one skootch to the center if kids would be drawn closer to parents, and one skootch to the outside if it would push them apart. The center is as far as you can go, although once you get to the center, you can move back if a situation sends you in the other direction.**

The situations appear in the text in the margin. (You may wish to add some situations of your own.) Comment on where the tweens are after the last situation is read. Invite them to suggest—still as either parents or tweens—the kinds of things that they believe would move them toward the center.

INTERACT

What Parents Do   Time: 15-25 minutes

Distribute photocopies of **Reproducible 2A, page 19**.

Say: On the sheet in your hands you'll see fifteen tasks that parents do. Some of those tasks are weightier or more

---

Stuff–Bottom Skootch:

☐ paper

☐ markers

☐ scissors

☐ tape

Bottom Skootch Statements:
1. *Parents sitting in on kids' conversation and getting chummy during a sleepover.*
2. *Parents agreeing to get lost while their tweens host a party at the house.*
3. *Preteen being honest with his or her feelings about a parent's outfit.*
4. *Parents deciding to divorce.*
5. *Attending worship and sitting together.*
6. *Attending worship together but parent giving permission for preteen to sit with friends.*
7. *Parents and preteens preparing and serving a meal at a homeless shelter.*
8. *Parent helping with homework.*
9. *Preteen asking to opt out of a family vacation in order to vacation with a friend.*
10. *Preteen not introducing parents to friends they run into at the mall.*
11. *Parent, worried about why preteen seems depressed, reading the preteen's journal.*
12. *Preteen offering to show parent some computer shortcuts.*

Stuff–What Parents Do:

☐ **Reproducible 2A, p. 19**

☐ pens or pencils

☐ *optional:* calculator

☐ *cool options:* pennies (100 per student), fifteen containers

---

important than others. You are going to decide which ones are the weightier tasks. You have 100 points that you have to distribute among the fifteen tasks on the sheet. You will indicate how important or weighty each task is by the number of points you write in column B beside that task. The B column must total 100 points exactly

Give them time to complete their assignment and then ask them to write in column C the names of persons who perform the five tasks to which they have given the most weight. Remind the tweens that these persons do not necessarily have to be their fathers or mothers.

Have the tweens assist you in counting up the points assigned by each class member. They can record the class totals in column D, and then in column E record the class average (divide column D by the number of tweens). Use calculators if available. Discuss the persons who have been listed in the tasks (column C) that the class has rated as most important or weightiest.

One Bible Dad: Good or Bad? Time: 10-15 minutes

Have the tweens turn to Ephesians 6:1-4 and read these verses aloud together. Invite their responses to these verses and expect that one response might be, "Do we have to obey our parents when what they tell us to do is wrong?" **Say: When the Bible speaks of fathers and mothers, it often is referring to ancestors in general. Even when it refers specifically to parents, it still implies those persons who are responsible for passing along the traditions and values of the culture or the faith. Living long and well is connected to living with the traditions of their ancestors, one of which is to put God at the center of their lives.**

Say: The law in Deuteronomy seems harsh and extreme to us. We can't justify it, but we can understand it. Remember life was difficult and family members working as a unit were essential. Parents also depended on children to care for them in their old age. With family as the basic unit and necessary for survival, there was no room for unruly children. It is important for us to be aware of this law before we look at a parent that Jesus talks about. Read Deuteronomy 21:18-21 as the tweens follow along in their Bibles.

Say: Now that you know how the law called for rebellious sons to be treated, let's listen to a story Jesus told about a father who was rebellious himself. To give his younger son his inheritance, the father would have had to give the older son his inheritance as well, which left the father with nothing, completely dependent on the older son since he's the one who stayed.

Cool Option for "What Parents Do" activity:

Place fifteen containers on a table. Number them 1 through 15. Give each participant 100 pennies. Have each tween decide the "weight" of each task by distributing pennies among the containers, marking on his or her sheet the number of pennies he or she put in each container.

Have participants help you count the total pennies in each container and then proceed as stated in the activity.

Stuff—One Bible Dad:

❏ **Reproducible 2B, p. 20**

❏ NRSV Bibles

❏ index cards

❏ markers

Fathers in Jesus' day would never have been caught running to greet a son; it simply wasn't done. A robe, a ring, and shoes were signs of belonging to a family, and the son who chose to abandon the family didn't deserve to have these things restored. And what about a father whose oldest son wasn't happy when his little brother, presumed dead, returned home? Withholding the stones was breaking the law. This was clearly a very bad father. Or was it?

Pass out photocopies of "One Rebellious Father, Two Rebellious Sons" (**Reproducible 2B, top of p. 20**) and use "body music" as accompaniment—tapping feet, patting legs, clapping hands, clicking fingers—for the telling of the story. Take turns saying the stanzas in rhythm.

Give each participant an index card and a marker and have him or her quickly write a number on the card, ranking the father on a scale of one to ten. Ask them to show their numbers and briefly discuss how they arrived at that rating.

Timing and Location Time: 10-15 minutes

Say: **In acting in general and comedy in particular, it's said that timing is everything. Actors or comedians need to sense just the right moment to move, deliver a line, or pause. In real estate, the rule you've probably heard is "location, location, location." Where you decide to build a house or set up a business makes a major difference when you go to sell the house or attempt to draw in customers. Whether you're on the giving or the receiving end of parenting, those two principles are true as well. When parents and kids need to communicate, where that happens and when it happens has a lot to do with the success of their communication.**

Ask the tweens to suggest topics that parents and tweens need to talk about together. List topics at the top of large sheets of paper—one topic per sheet. Be sure that one of the topics gets at the issue of faith. Tape these on the wall or place them on the floor or a table. Have the tweens circulate among these sheets of paper, adding specific locations and times or occasions where that topic might most effectively be discussed, and things that the tweens might do to help parents help them. Encourage them to work quickly, and then review each of the sheets and allow comments from tweens.

Have them complete the Reality Check (**Reproducible 2B, bottom of p. 20**) based on this conversation.

Stuff–Timing and Location:

❏ **Reproducible 2B, p. 20**

❏ large sheets of paper

❏ markers

❏ pens or pencils

❏ *optional:* tape

Parenting and Kidding

- ❏ "Affirmation of Us" poster, p. 64

- ❏ masking tape or pushpins

Stuff–Body Language:

- ❏ paper

- ❏ pens or pencils

- ❏ scissors

DEPART   Time: 2 minutes

Mount the "Affirmation of Us" poster. Following the prayer lead the group in repeating the affirmation.

Pray: O God, in those moments when we expect those who parent us to be superhuman but consider them to be subhuman, remind us gently that they are, like us, only human. You know it's not easy to be a preteen and not easy to be a parent, so teach us to make things easier for one another. Thank you for Jesus, who helps us see how as parents and kids we are to treat each other. Amen.

PLAN PLUS

Body Language   Time: 10 minutes

Extra time? Try this variation on charades. Write the phrases below on slips of paper. Have the tweens take turns drawing slips of paper and assuming a position, facial expression, or action that conveys what is on the paper. The others will write that person's name on a sheet of paper, and beside it what they think that person's body language is saying. When all have had a turn, compare lists to see if they have been reading the body language accurately. If you have more tweens than phrases, gather the slips of paper and have those who have not had a turn draw one.

Body Language Phrases

- You are so lame!
- You're embarrassing me!
- We've heard that before.
- I don't believe you said that!
- Boring!
- I'm in love!
- Pop quiz.
- I fixed your favorite meal!
- Liar!
- I don't want to talk about it now.
- I want to tell you but don't know how.
- Please? Just this once?
- I'm late again.
- You're late again.
- I am so disappointed.
- I give up.
- Ooo! Ooo! Pick me!
- I'm so proud of you!
- You can't make me talk!

Explain that often tweens or parents interpret the body language rather than the words.

Reproducible 2A

A. What Do Parents Do?

	B. Weight you give this task.	C. Who parents you? For the five tasks you weighted the highest, name the person(s) who parents you in this way.	D. Weight class gives this task.	E. Average Column D divided by number in class.
1. Take care of you or get you to the doctor when you are sick.				
2. Check to make sure that your homework is done and done properly.				
3. Help you when you are having problems with your homework.				
4. Earn a living in order to provide for your basic needs.				
5. Prepare meals.				
6. Listen to you when you need to talk.				
7. Congratulate you for little successes and major accomplishments.				
8. Keep track of your comings and goings, know where you are at all times.				
9. Insist that you get enough sleep.				
10. Provide transportation for you or make arrangements for transportation.				
11. Take you to church and make sure your faith is being nurtured.				
12. Show interest and, if necessary, concern regarding the people you hang with.				
13. Answer your questions about the changes you experience as you mature.				
14. Give you hugs and let you know that you are loved.				
15. Encourage you to continue when something you've attempted becomes difficult.				
Total 100				

© 2005 Abingdon Press. Permission is granted for the original purchaser to reproduce this page for use in the local church or educational setting. Copyright notice must be included on all reproductions.

One Rebellious Father/Two Rebellious Sons

One father had
two different sons.
"Hey, Daddy dear!"
said younger one.
"I cannot wait
until you die.
Give me my due
and I'll say bye."

So father split
up all he had.
The younger son
said, "See ya, Dad!"
He traveled off
with his demands,
and wasted all,
in foreign lands.

A famine came—
what would he do?
Go find some work
to see him through.
Thus feeding pigs
was his employ—
an unclean task
for Jewish boy.

So hungry was
this wasteful dude,
he almost ate
the piggy food.
"What have I done?
Oh me, oh my!
Dad's hired hands
have more than I!"

"I'll head for home—
that's what I'll do;
say, 'Dad I've sinned
'gainst God and you!
Don't call me son,
I've been a jerk!
Don't give me love.
But how 'bout work?'"

He practiced well
what he would say,
and headed home
that very day.
Before he neared
the house, his dad
saw him and ran.
Such love he had!

He hugged him close,
gave him a kiss.
Son said, "I'm not
deserving this!"
Son started to
recite his spiel,
but Dad broke in
with joy and zeal.

"Slaves, bring a robe,
shoes for his feet,
rings for his hands,
and then let's eat!
The fatted calf!
Let food abound!
My son was lost,
but now is found!"

To older son
who stayed at home,
cared for his dad,
and didn't roam,
a slave reports
on all the noise:
"Your dad again
has both his boys!"

The older son
was mighty peeved.
Said, "This is not
to be believed!
I'll not go in
and greet this louse!"
His father pled,
"Come in the house!"

"No way!" he said.
"I've slaved for you.
Done everything
you asked me to.
Not once have you
rewarded me.
It isn't fair!
Inequity!

"He took your gift—
just hear him laugh—
spent it on sin!
You kill the calf!"
"My son, my son,
please get a grip,
What's mine is yours.
You need a trip!

"Our only choice?
To celebrate!
The lost is found!
Is this not great?
It's just as though
this son was dead.
So lighten up!
He lives instead!"

Reality Check	Where to talk	When to talk	How to make the most of the time
1. My feelings and thoughts about church and faith			
2. What's going on with my friends.			
3. How things are going at school.			
4. Growing up and changes in my body.			
5. Other activities in which I'm involved.			

© 2005 Abingdon Press. Permission is granted for the original purchaser to reproduce this page for use in the local church or educational setting. Copyright notice must be included on all reproductions.

Live It! My Family

SIBLING RIVALRY

THE POINT

Our faith, evidenced in compromise and forgiveness, can have a positive influence in dealing with sibling rivalry.

THE SKILLS

Tweens will
• understand sibling characteristics.
• understand acceptance of differences.
• learn about commitment to sibling relationships.

THE BIBLE

Genesis 32:9-12, 22-32; 33:1-10; John 13:34-35

THE PLAN

PREPARE yourself

Squabbling among brothers and sisters is normal. However, constant arguing, putting one another down, and fighting that can create harmful situations are matters of real concern.

There are several reasons for sibling rivalry. At times it occurs because brothers and sisters fight to get their parents' attention. Sometimes it is to show power or superiority over the other sibling.

Tweens are well into developing their own personality and characteristics such as language expressions, the way they dress,

---

PREPARE your session

Stuff to collect:
- [ ] NRSV Bibles
- [ ] index cards
- [ ] pens or pencils
- [ ] teen magazines and catalogs
- [ ] glue
- [ ] scissors
- [ ] soft drink bottle
- [ ] paper
- [ ] small, six-sided box
- [ ] markers
- [ ] *optional:* craft items
- [ ] masking tape or pushpins
- [ ] pennies (*optional:* buttons, stickers, or small pieces of paper)
- [ ] **Reproducible 3A, p. 27**
- [ ] **Reproducible 3B, p. 28**
- [ ] **"Affirmation of Us" poster, p. 64**

For cool options:
- [ ] paper
- [ ] markers
- [ ] pens or pencils

Stuff to do:
1. Make photocopies of Reproducibles 3A and 3B.

and their choice of friends. Sometimes brothers and sisters are seen as obstacles in this development. Often parents place responsibilities on the older to take care of the younger, the younger to follow the older. These responsibilities can become heavy burdens for the sibling to carry.

In the Scriptures for this lesson, Jacob and Esau had fallen out of favor of one another because Jacob had tricked their father into giving Jacob the inheritance of his older brother, Esau. After years of separation, God directed Jacob to return to his country and Esau. Jacob sent presents by his servants ahead, hoping to please Esau, and they reunited on good terms.

GATHER

I Like, I Hate Time: 5 minutes

Hand out index cards. Have each tween write on a card the name of a brother or sister and two of that sibling's characteristics—one characteristic describing something the tween appreciates, and one characteristic that the tween dislikes. If a tween has no brothers or sisters, have him or her name a relative that would be from the correct age group; someone he or she spends time with routinely. (There are other activities in this lesson where he or she will need to refer to this person in place of a sibling.)

Have the tweens place their cards in a pile. Ask for volunteers to take one card at a time and read it to the group. Continue until all of the cards have been read.

Ask: What are some things we heard that are in common among us? What did we hear that was unique?

Picture Perfect Time: 10 minutes

Have a variety of teen magazines and catalogs. Ask the tweens to cut out pictures of faces, bodies, hair, clothes, and so forth to create a picture of a sibling they would like to have. Ask them to write around the finished picture the characteristics they would want the perfect sibling to have.

 If you do not have a sufficient number of magazines and catalogs available, use one of these cool options.

Cool Option: Ask tweens to draw their ideal siblings.

Stuff–I Like, I Hate:

❑ index cards

❑ pens or pencils

Stuff–Picture Perfect:

❑ teen magazines and catalogs

❑ scissors

❑ paper

❑ glue

❑ *cool options:* paper, markers, pens or pencils

Cool Option: Ask tweens to make a list of characteristics of their ideal siblings.

Say: In a perfect world we could have ideal brothers and sisters; but in reality, no one is perfect. And believe it or not, things we think would be perfect sometimes turn out to be not so easy to live with.

INTERACT

Spin the Bottle and Talk Time: 5-10 minutes

Let everyone sit on the floor in a circle. Place a soft drink bottle on the floor in the middle of the circle. Let the tweens take turns spinning the bottle. The person to whom the bottle is pointing tells something about a sibling—name, age, physical description, and a conflict they have had. Then he or she spins the bottle for the next turn.

Read the Bible Time: 15 minutes

Say: We have been talking about the conflicts we have had with our brothers and sisters. What do you think would happen if the conflict got out of hand and escalated to something terrible? The Bible tells us the story of two brothers that had a devastating conflict. Let's see what happened.

Divide the tweens into six teams and assign them passages of Scripture: Team 1: Genesis 27:5-17; Team 2: Genesis 27:18-30; Team 3: Genesis 27:41-44; Team 4: Genesis 32:9-12; Team 5: Genesis 32:22-32; Team 6: Genesis 33:1-10.

Have each team tell the important parts of the story in their own words. Each team has a time limit of one minute to report in.

Ask: Why do you think Esau forgave Jacob? What do you think would have happened if Esau had still been angry? How do you think Jacob felt after being forgiven? What is the hardest part about forgiving someone?

Cool Option: Let each group act out their part of the story. Encourage them to ham it up, but they have a one minute time limit for their presentation so they will have to "fast forward" through their presentation.

Stuff–Spin the Bottle and Talk:

❑ soft drink bottle

Stuff–Read the Bible:

❑ NRSV Bibles

❑ paper

❑ pens or pencils

❑ small, six-sided box

❑ pens, pencils, or
   markers

❑ *optional:* craft items to
   decorate box

Just Between You and Me! Time: 10 minutes

Pass out photocopies of **Reproducible 3A, p. 27**. Ask for volunteers to read the parts. After the reading ask the following questions:

1. Do you think it's fair for Jonathan to tell Randy what to do?

2. Why do you suppose Jonathan is asked to take responsibility for Randy?

3. Do you think the boys are different ages? If so, what ages would they be? What if they are twins? Why would Jonathan be asked to help out?

4. Since Randy and Jonathan are both tired of the situation, how do you think they could work it out between themselves?

5. What should Randy and Jonathan say to their parents about the situation? What could be done differently?

Options for Working It Out Time 5-10 minutes

Have the tweens help prepare a small box by writing one of the following words on each side of the box to create six different sides: *negotiate*, *forgive*, *apologize*, *ignore*, *help*, and *argue*. Allow the tweens to add any extra decorations they desire.

Read each of the following situations. Have the tweens take turns tossing the box in the air, then check the word that appears on the top of the box when it lands and tell how the situation can be changed by doing that action. Have the box tossed two or more times for each situation. Afterward, ask the group which option for working it out would be the best option.

Situation 1: Although David is older than Marc, they can wear the same size clothes. David needed a clean shirt to wear to a church youth gathering and took Marc's favorite shirt to wear without asking Marc. Marc is very upset about it.

Situation 2: Mary and her twin sister Betty want to go to the movie Saturday. When they get to the movie, an argument breaks out. Betty wants to see a movie with a PG-13 rating. Mary says no because they are not allowed without their mom and dad giving permission. Mary says they have to go to a movie with a G rating.

Situation 3: Sam found out that his sister has told a girl at school that Sam likes her. Sam is very embarrassed and hurt by this "unsolicited" help.

Situation 4: Cruz did not complete his homework and got into trouble with his teacher. Later Cruz finds out that his younger brother has not only told Cruz's parents what happened, he has been exaggerating about it and making it sound worse than it was.

Situation 5: Jennifer is trying to study for a test tomorrow. Jamie, her little sister, keeps running into Jennifer's room and poking Jennifer in the ribs to make Jennifer chase her. Finally Jennifer gets mad and slaps at Jamie. Now Jamie is screaming to her parents that Jennifer is trying to hit her.

DEPART Time: 10 minutes

Read John 13:34-35.

Pass out photocopies of "Ten Christian Commitments" (**Reproducible 3B, p. 28**). Have a volunteer read the first commitment.

Ask: Can any of you give an example of something you can do with or for your brother or sister to live by this commitment?

Ask for volunteers to read each commitment and ask for examples of each.

Together repeat the "Affirmation of Us."

Pray: Dear God, please help us to find ways to relate to our brothers and sisters. Help us to have patience when we need to be patient. Help us to be forgiving when we need to forgive. Help us to act in kind and caring ways. Thank you, God, for helping us. Amen.

Stuff–Depart:

❑ **Reproducible 3B, p. 28**

❑ **"Affirmation of Us" poster, p. 64**

❑ **NRSV Bibles**

❑ masking tape or pushpins

Teacher Tip: Reproducible 3B will be used at the end of lessons 3 through 6. Each week there will be a different question to ask as a result of that day's subject.

Stuff-Kindness Pays:

❏ pennies (twenty pennies per tween plus additional pennies to give out during class)

Teacher Tip: You may wish to use buttons, stickers, or even small pieces of paper instead of pennies. You will still need twenty per tween and an additional supply to give out during class.

Kindness Pays Time: 5 minutes (beginning and end of class)

Conflicts between siblings can be lessened when siblings learn to relate to one another with the same courtesies that are generally extended to most of the people we encounter.

At the beginning of class, give each tween twenty pennies. Explain that more pennies can be earned during the remainder of class time by being courteous. Be certain everyone understands that these ways must occur naturally and not be staged. When you witness a tween doing one of the following, give him or her a penny.

1. Giving sincere encouragement to a fellow tween.
2. Performing kind or helpful actions.
3. Offering a sincere apology.
4. Graciously accepting an apology.
5. Not interrupting when someone is talking.
6. Listening politely.
7. Respecting a person's feelings.
8. Allowing free expression of personal opinions.

Explain that pennies can be confiscated if you witness a tween doing one of the following:

1. Not reciprocating with kind or helpful actions.
2. Insulting or putting down someone.
3. Interrupting.
4. Not apologizing when the circumstances call for an apology.
5. Performing any rude behavior that shows disrespect.

Without the tweens knowing it, add the following penalties:
1. Anyone who tattles loses five pennies.
2. Anyone who refuses to admit they did something wrong loses five pennies.

At the end of class, have everyone count their pennies.

Say: In our class we have made an extra effort to be kind, respectful, and caring. You can see by the pennies you accumulated that kindness pays! It is the same way in our families. By treating our brothers and sisters with the same courtesies, conflicts don't occur as often, or they are not as severe, or they do not last as long. It takes an extra effort sometimes, but it pays to try.

Reproducible 3A

Just Between You and Me

Father: Okay you guys, it's time to get up!

Mother: Yes, I've got your breakfast sitting on the table.

Jonathan: Okay, Dad. I'm up.

Father: Randy, are you getting up too? Randy?

Randy: Okay, okay, I'm getting up!

Jonathan: Randy, why do you do this every morning? Dad has to yell at us every morning!

Randy: He wasn't yelling at you, so why do you care?

Jonathan: Because he will blame me if you don't get up and get downstairs for breakfast.

Mother: We have to get on our way now, boys, so hurry up and get started with your breakfast. And Jonathan, be sure that Randy puts on clean clothes and brushes his teeth.

Jonathan: Okay, Mom. Let's go, Randy! NOW!

Randy: You're not my boss, so stop yelling at me! Just between you and me, I'm tired of you bossing me around.

Jonathan: Well, I'm tired of it too! When you don't do as you're told, Dad expects me to make you behave.

Father: Hey, boys! What's going on here? Didn't we ask you to get downstairs to eat breakfast?

© 2005 Abingdon Press. Permission is granted for the original purchaser to reproduce this page for use in the local church or educational setting. Copyright notice must be included on all reproductions.

"I give you a new commandment, that you love one another. Just as I have loved you, you also should love one another. By this everyone will know that you are my disciples, if you have love for one another." (John 13:34-35)

Ten Christian Commitments in My Home!

1. I will consider the needs of my brothers and sisters.

2. I will share my belongings.

3. I will listen intently and politely to what others have to say.

4. I will not brag constantly about my accomplishments.

5. I will say please and thank you.

6. I will praise the accomplishments of others in my home.

7. I will not put anyone down.

8. I will accept that others may not wish to do, or like, those things that I like.

9. I will respect others' rights of privacy.

10. I will control my temper and find acceptable ways to express my anger.

© 2005 Abingdon Press. Permission is granted for the original purchaser to reproduce this page for use in the local church or educational setting. Copyright notice must be included on all reproductions.

ENTRANCES INTO MY FAMILY

THE POINT

Our faith prepares us to respond in appropriate ways as our family dramas shift with the entrance of new characters.

THE SKILLS

Tweens will
• develop the ability to communicate feelings regarding the new family member.
• learn acceptance of his or her own new role and the role of the new member in the family.
• develop the capability of establishing a healthy relationship with the new family member.

THE BIBLE

John 19:25b-27; 1 Peter 4:8-11

THE PLAN

PREPARE yourself

New family members can be traumatic to existing family members at any age, but to a tween, it can be a disaster! Whether it's a newborn sibling, a foster or adopted child, a stepparent, or an elderly grandparent moving into the house, their lives are going to change forever. The way in which the parent or parents communicate and prepare for the arrival can make all of the difference. Preparation and communication are the key. However there are no guarantees. The best laid plans may not be enough.

PREPARE your session

Stuff to collect:
- [ ] NRSV Bibles
- [ ] paper
- [ ] pens or pencils
- [ ] large sheet of paper and marker, markerboard and erasable marker, or chalkboard and chalk
- [ ] markers
- [ ] construction paper
- [ ] scissors
- [ ] glue
- [ ] craft supplies such as glitter
- [ ] small bag
- [ ] masking tape or pushpins
- [ ] **Reproducible 4A, p. 35**
- [ ] **Reproducible 4B, p. 36**
- [ ] **Reproducible 3B, p. 28**
- [ ] **"Affirmation of Us" poster, p. 64**

For ☀ cool options:
- [ ] plastic foam forms; craft supplies such as art paper, gel markers, fabric, paint, and string; toothpicks; straws

Stuff to do:
1. Make photocopies of Reproducibles 3B, 4A and 4B.
2. Create list of codes for family member types (see "My Family" activity).
3. Cut five geometric shapes out of construction paper per each group of three tweens (see "Create a Family" activity).
4. Cut apart roleplay situations (Reproducible 4B) and put in small bag (see "Entrances Into My Family Roleplay" activity).

As a teacher, you will want to be careful that the tweens don't get out of control expressing the family problems that have taken place in their lives, but at the same time, give them an opportunity to identify categories instead. "Loss of space," "caregiver," "limited time with parent(s)," "fewer outdoor activities" are helpful ways of looking at situations. The key is to point out the situation, not the person.

These categories are less provoking than specific events such as, "My stepdad makes me go to bed early because he wants time with his own children" or, "I have to stay home and watch the baby." So plan on ways to keep the tone less challenging and have sets of questions to ask to draw out responses in a safe manner.

John 19:25b-27 tells us about how Jesus from the cross asked his disciple John to take his mother Mary into his home and there take care of her. The disciple took Mary into his own home.

Change will always take place in our lives. How we deal with it depends on preparation and communication. Help your tweens understand how Jesus asks us all to be disciples and care about each other, even by sometimes accepting new members into the family.

In **1 Peter 4:8-11**, Peter tells us to stand ready for judgment. We are to maintain constant love for one another and to be good managers of God's gifts. Each family member brings gifts, talents, and strengths. Together, the family can serve God as it is intended. Each one, as a good manager of God's different gifts, must use for the good of others the special gift he or she has received from God.

It is very important for tweens to understand that each member of the family is valuable to the family. When different gifts and abilities are used in harmony, the family experiences well-being and a feeling of permanence.

GATHER

My Family   Time: 5 minutes

As the tweens arrive, have them write down on a sheet of paper all of their immediate family members, being certain to name anyone who lives in their home. Have them identify who they are: (B) for brother, (SB) for stepbrother, (S) for sister, (M) for mother or (SM) for stepmother, (D) for dad or (SD) for stepdad, (A) for aunt, (GM) for grandmother, and so forth. Have this list of

Stuff—My Family:

❏ paper

❏ pens or pencils

❏ large sheet of paper and marker, markerboard and erasable marker, or chalkboard and chalk

identifying codes already written on a chalkboard, markerboard, or large sheet of paper so they can select from a complete list of family members and know how to identify them.

Every Family Has Changes   Time: 5 minutes

On the lists they made in the previous activity, have the tweens circle all of the family members who have entered their lives since they were born and then write next to the identifying code how long ago this occurred. Then have the tweens share their responses. On the list of identifying codes you prepared for the previous activity, put a checkmark beside the appropriate spot for each tween who has one of these "new members."

Give each tween two pieces of paper. On one have them write "good" and on the other "bad." Then read down the completed list of new family members and have them vote by holding up their choices as to whether this addition was seen as "good" or "bad." List the vote count beside each item on the list. Assure everyone that honesty is very important and that privacy is guaranteed. This allows the tween to identify how he or she feels without risk. It also shows that they aren't alone—people constantly experience entrances into their lives.

INTERACT

Create a Family   Time: 10 minutes

Divide your class into teams of three members each. Give each team five different shapes cut out of construction paper and glue. Have them glue the shapes into a "family shape." Give them markers, glitter, and/or other craft supplies and let them decorate their family shape.

When done, have them describe each shape as a member of a family. Then give each team a new but different additional geometric piece to add to their family shape and see what they do with it.

Ask: Who is the family member you added? How did the addition of the new shape really change your family structure? What members were most common in every family? What was unusual in any of the families?

Say: When we think of families, we often think of a mother, father, and children. However, in today's world, that may not be the case.

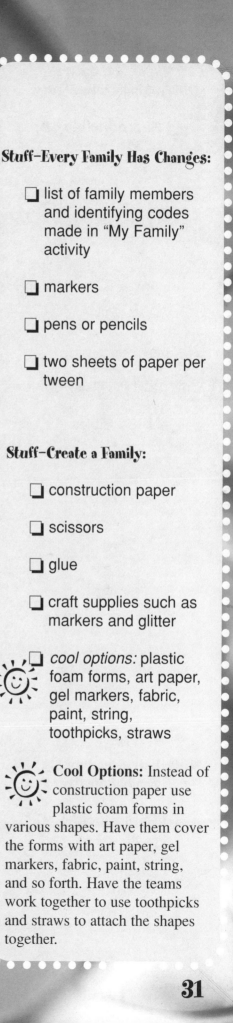

Stuff—Every Family Has Changes:

☐ list of family members and identifying codes made in "My Family" activity

☐ markers

☐ pens or pencils

☐ two sheets of paper per tween

Stuff—Create a Family:

☐ construction paper

☐ scissors

☐ glue

☐ craft supplies such as markers and glitter

☐ *cool options: plastic foam forms, art paper, gel markers, fabric, paint, string, toothpicks, straws*

Cool Options: Instead of construction paper use plastic foam forms in various shapes. Have them cover the forms with art paper, gel markers, fabric, paint, string, and so forth. Have the teams work together to use toothpicks and straws to attach the shapes together.

Entrances Into My Family

❑ **Reproducible 4A, p. 35**

Stuff–Read the Bible:

❑ NRSV Bibles

Stuff–Entrances Into My Family Roleplay:

❑ **Reproducible 4B, p. 36**

❑ scissors

❑ small bag

A Modern-Day Story Time: 10-20 minutes

Pass out photocopies of "A Modern-Day Story" (**Reproducible 4A, p. 35**). Ask for two volunteers to read the parts of David and Mother. **Say: This story has two possible outcomes. You may pick the path you want to take, A or B.**

Have the readers select a path. Ask them to read the parts for that path. When they finish, ask them to read the parts for the other path. **Ask: What was David worried about? How did his worries grow out of control? How did the mother handle David's worries? Was there anything else she could have said? Which path was the better path? Do we usually have two paths to choose from in most situations? What can we do to choose the better path?**

Read the Bible Time: 15 minutes

• John 19:25b-27: Have tweens act as if they standing at the feet of Jesus on the cross. Have a tween read the part of Jesus. Ask two tweens to act out the parts of Mary and John. Encourage them to think of what John might have said to Mary and what Mary might have said to John. How would other bystanders have acted?

• 1 Peter 4:8-11: Ask four readers to take turns reading each verse.

Ask: What is supposed to be constant? What are we to do with the gifts we have received from God? What does this Scripture tells us about how we are to treat each other?

Say: Having a new family member enter your personal family does change the family structure. But the biggest difference occurs within your own mind and heart. Just as Jesus asked his disciple to include his mother in his family, we should look for the positive results of a new member in our families.

Entrances Into My Family Roleplay Time: 15 minutes

Make a photocopy of **Reproducible 4B, p. 36**.

Divide the tweens into four teams. Cut apart the roleplay situations and put them in a small bag.

Have each team draw out one roleplay. Instruct the teams to read their situation and consider all the possible outcomes. Have the teams select one outcome and act out their situation for the rest of the class.

After each roleplay, **Ask: What were some of the outcomes you considered? What was the hardest part of the situation to deal with? How could this situation be handled constructively?**

DEPART

Ten Christian Commitments Time: 5-8 minutes

Pass out photocopies of "Ten Christian Commitments" (**Reproducible 3B, p. 28**). Have a volunteer read the first commitment.

Ask: Can any of you give an example of how you can use this commitment with a new family member? Give some examples to help your tweens with this. Ask for other volunteers to read each of the commitments and ask for examples of how each can be used with a new family member.

Together repeat the "Affirmation of Us." **Pray: Dear God, we ask that you show us how we can help and accept persons who are becoming new members of our family. Help us to be patient and kind as we experience the change and get to know our new family. Help us to remember that even Mary entered a new family. Please bless each of our families and each person in our families. Amen.**

PLAN PLUS

Dealing Out the Chores Time: 15 minutes

Use the following activity to help your tweens recognize the important role that each person plays as a member of a dynamic nuclear family.

Divide the class into groups of between four and eight persons. Each group will contain a father and/or mother, two siblings (male and/or female), and a least one grandparent or other member such as a foster or adopted tween or a cousin. Have each tween decide which member of the family he or she will be.

Ask each group to make a list of family responsibilities. Encourage them to consider everything that is needed to maintain their lives as a family. As a family decide three tasks that each family member should be responsible for on a daily, weekly, or monthly period of time. Remind the tweens that the tasks should be those which that member would normally be expected to perform.

Entrances Into My Family

Teacher Tip: Reproducible 3B will be used again next week and each week through 6. Each week there will be a different question to ask as a result of that day's subject.

Types of Responsibilities:

• Has financial (bread-winner) responsibility
• Handles paying the bills
• Drives the car for carpool
• Decides when to go to church
• Cuts the grass
• Makes final selection of new clothes
• Pays for new clothes
• Does the laundry
• Does housework
• Decides which television programs can be viewed
• Buys the groceries
• Decides what car to buy
• Washes the dishes
• Washes the car
• Says grace at the table

Have the groups read off from their lists what has been decided.

Say: When everyone takes care of his or her responsibilities, there is harmony in the family. Just as the spokes on a bicycle wheel are individually not able to hold the rim together, neither is it possible for only one person in the family to do everything a family needs. Each person is important. Each person plays a vital role in the family.

Ask: Are there ever times when responsibilities need to change?

Name Train   Time: 5-7 minutes

Ask everyone to sit in a circle. Ask everyone to think of the different members that families have.

Begin by having the first player name a category of family member that he or she has—for example, "mother." Have the next player call out a name and repeat the one before—for example, "father, mother." Continue around the circle having the players add a new name and calling out all the others that have already been said. Explain that a name different from the one just called must be used.

Stuff–Name Train:

❑ none

Reproducible 4A
A Modern-Day Story

Mother: David, I need to talk to you about something that's very important to us both. Can you sit with me and let's talk about it?

David: Sure, Mom. What's up?

Mother: Well, David, it's been a long time since your dad and I divorced. In the past few weeks I've been seeing a man that I met at work. It's not serious right now, but he is a nice man.

Which path—**A** or **B**?

• •

Path A

David: Mom! How come I'm finding out about this now? Why didn't you tell me before now that you are seeing someone?

Mother: David, I didn't think it was necessary to tell you until I thought it was getting to be a serious relationship. If it's not serious, it is no different from anyone else I see on a daily basis.

David: I feel like you're going to start going out with him and I will have to be alone. That's not fair!

Mother: David, this is not going to change anything. Michael, the man I'm seeing, is such a nice man. You will meet him some time soon and see just how nice he is.

David: Yes, but it will have to change things. After all, you will be spending more time with him than with me, won't you?

Mother: It's true that we will spend time together, but you can be with us a lot.

David: Then everything will be different. He will want the two of you do things, and I will be left out. And what if it gets serious? What if you get married? I already have a dad!

Mother: Why can't you let me be happy for a while?

Path B

David: Will it change the time we have together if you are seeing him?

Mother: I'm sure it will change some things, but I hope that you and he can get along. He loves to fish, and you know you do too! I think you will have a lot in common and can do a lot of things that I can't do. What do you think?

David: Well, it sounds okay, but I don't want to lose the time we have together.

Mother: That won't change. We will actually have more time to do things since there are so many outdoor activities that I can't do with you. I'm asking you to meet him, spend some time with him, and see for yourself what it will be like. What do you think?

David: I'll give it a try, Mom.

© 2005 Abingdon Press. Permission is granted for the original purchaser to reproduce this page for use in the local church or educational setting. Copyright notice must be included on all reproductions.

Reproducible 4B

Entrances Into My Family Roleplays

1. Matt, who is eleven, has just been told by his father that Grandpa is moving in with them because of Grandpa's failing health. His father says that Matt must give up his large bedroom, since it is next to the hall bathroom, and move into a much smaller one. Grandpa needs to be close to the bathroom because he can't walk very far. Matt has always loved his Grandpa.

a. How will Matt now feel about his Grandpa?
b. What will Matt's response be to this situation?
c. What might be some options for Matt?

2. Tanisha has been the only child of her parents for eleven years. They live in a very modest two bedroom home and most of their entertainment is the TV and a drive to the park on weekends. Mom has told Tanisha that she is pregnant and will be having the baby in five months. As a result, there will have to be some "belt-tightening" because of their financial situation. Up to this time, Tanisha has had a nice weekly allowance and few responsibilities around the home.

a. What are some of the things Tanisha will face with the baby's arrival?
b. What new responsibilities might Tanisha have because of the new baby?
c. How might Tanisha react to the announcement?

3. Brad has lived with his mother, who is a single parent, for eight years. Brad's father died when he was about four years old. Recently Brad's mother married a man with two children of his own—a girl who is fifteen, and a boy who is five. Brad and his mom have moved into his stepdad's house, and he must share a room with his new stepbrother. Brad is upset with this situation.

a. What are the possible reasons for Brad being upset?
b. How will Brad likely treat his new stepbrother?
c. What should Brad do to make the situation more bearable?

4. Tyrone was adopted when he was four years old. He has been the only child that the Wilson's have. Occasionally, the Wilson's have brought into their care foster children who have been abused. The Wilson's have decided to adopt another child about the same age as Tyrone.

a. What might be the changes in Tyrone's life with this addition to the family?
b. Would the changes be different if it were a boy rather than a girl?
c. What are the potential positive outcomes of this addition?

© 2005 Abingdon Press. Permission is granted for the original purchaser to reproduce this page for use in the local church or educational setting. Copyright notice must be included on all reproductions.

EXITS FROM MY FAMILY

THE POINT

Our faith prepares us to respond in appropriate ways as our family dramas shift with the exit of familiar characters.

THE SKILLS

Tweens will
• develop the ability to express feelings about the exits that take place in their lives.
• find comfort in helping others who experience exits.
• find ways to accept exits as part of their life.
• recognize that their hurt, anger, fear, and sadness are acceptable feelings.

THE BIBLE

Psalm 130:1, 5; John 14:27; 19:25b-27

THE PLAN

PREPARE yourself

One of the most difficult experiences that any of us face is the loss of someone we love. As a tween, the first loss will hurt deeply, and whether your tweens have experienced it or not, you can help them prepare for a family exit. Death, divorce, a sibling going off to college, a parent or sibling going off to war, and hospitalization are forms of exits that surely we all face at one

PREPARE your session

Stuff to collect:
- ❑ NRSV Bibles
- ❑ large sheet of paper and marker or chalkboard and chalk
- ❑ index cards
- ❑ pens or pencils
- ❑ paper
- ❑ markers
- ❑ tempera paint
- ❑ paintbrushes
- ❑ manila file folders
- ❑ craft supplies
- ❑ glue
- ❑ paper punch
- ❑ yard or cord
- ❑ masking tape or pushpins
- ❑ salad spinner
- ❑ six-inch paper plates
- ❑ paper towels
- ❑ safety pins
- ❑ candles
- ❑ drip protectors
- ❑ matches
- ❑ *optional:* penlights
- ❑ **"Affirmation of Us" poster, p. 64**
- ❑ **Reproducible 3B, p. 28**
- ❑ **Reproducible 5A, p. 43**
- ❑ **Reproducible 5B, p. 44**

For ☼ cool options:
- ❑ weeds, leaves, ferns, and grasses
- ❑ green, black, and yellow tempera paint and paintbrushes
- ❑ brightly colored art foam

Stuff to do:
1. Make photocopies of Reproducibles 3B, 5A and 5B.
2. Make list of possible family exit experiences (see "Exit Experiences" activity).
3. Select type of Reflection Journal covers and gather craft supplies (see "Reflection Journal" activity).
4. Check on your church's policy on the use of lit candles (see "Pray for Each Other" activity).

Teacher Tip: Most tweens have already experienced either some loss in their lives or secretly fear such a loss. Some will not have had major losses. Help tweens without major losses to think about friends and/or extended family members who may have had such losses.

Some tweens may now be experiencing separation or loss of friends due to entering middle school.

Stuff—Exit Experiences:

❏ large sheet of paper and marker or chalkboard and chalk

❏ index cards

❏ pens or pencils

Teacher Tip: To ensure privacy no names should be used on the cards.

time or another. For some it is the death of a pet that has been considered part of the family.

As children age their reactions to loss vary. Tweens may feel their despair longer than a preschool child. They may feel angry and disillusioned. They may lose self-esteem and generally distrust everything. Sometimes extreme behaviors, from doing everything they are asked to do without question to breaking all the rules, result from their attempt to deal with the trauma. Depression becomes a real concern.

Being able to openly talk about these experiences of loss is the first step in dealing with the trauma associated with loss. Look within your own life and pull out the feelings that you may have experienced. What could anyone have said that would have made the pain go away? Nothing. But being able to tell someone about your hurt and disappointment may have lessened the pain. Be prepared to hear some heart-wrenching experiences, but take the time to listen. Read the verses in **Psalm 130**, a prayer for help, which tells us that even in despair, asking for God's help can help us bear the pain.

In **John 14:27**, Jesus reassures his disciples that he leaves them peace and tells them not to be worried and upset; he tells them not to be afraid. Reassure your tweens that their Christian faith will give them the strength to endure. In **John 19:25b-27**, Jesus asks his mother and the disciple John to help each other to endure his death together. We can learn from this that seeking God's help, and that of others, is a means of dealing with the exits in our lives. Often we can help ourselves through helping others.

GATHER

Exit Experiences Time: 5 minutes

Before class make a list of possible exits for your tweens to look at. Include death, divorce, different kinds of extended separations, moving, and hospitalization. Talk with the tweens about each one. Help them to explore any possible scenario and write it on the list.

Give each tween a few index cards. Encourage each person to find a place in the room where he or she can privately write on the card any of the exits that they have experienced or might someday experience—one exit per card. You too should fill out cards.

Gather the cards and have a tween separate them according to the exit. Have another tween write the number of cards in each category on a large sheet of paper or chalkboard to show the tweens that they aren't alone in experiencing these departures in their lives.

Drawing on Experience Time: 15 minutes

Have your tweens create a picture of an exit that they have experienced. Have available crayons, markers, and paint in bright, bold, and dark colors. If they prefer not to draw the experience, encourage them to use color to illustrate how they felt about the experience. Ask for volunteers to explain what they have created to represent the departure in their life. **Ask: What emotions do you see in what your friends have created?**

Say: When we have exits in our life we feel a loss. Sometimes we feel like crying and maybe we do cry. Sometimes we are angry and can't even say why. Sometimes we are confused and don't understand why things had to happen this way. Sometimes we feel lonely and don't know what to do. All of these feelings are normal. It helps to talk about your feelings. The person you talk with may have already experienced that kind of loss and can help you. But at the very least, you know that person cares about what you are going through. Always talk with someone; you don't have to go it alone. Prayer is talking with God. God always cares.

INTERACT

It Looks Different From Here Time: 15 minutes

Divide the class into four teams. Give each team a copy of "It Looks Different From Here" (**Reproducible 5A, p. 43**). Assign each team one of the scenarios. Ask for team members to take turns reading the scenario and the possible reactions. For each reaction, ask each team to answer the question, "What would happen if this were the reaction?" Have one person on each team act as a scribe and write down all the possible outcomes.

Encourage the tweens to talk freely. Be aware that some may still be reluctant to be open. Even though most tweens love to talk, not all are comfortable talking in a public situation about private feelings. Encouraging humor in some of the responses may help reduce self-consciousness or any discomfort a tween may be feeling.

When each group is finished, ask for a volunteer from each group to read their scenario to everyone and read the possible outcomes as if they were a continuation of the story.

Exits From My Family

Stuff-Drawing on Experience:

❑ paper

❑ markers

❑ tempera paint and paintbrushes

Teacher Tip: Encourage abstract art. Often abstract art allows us to express emotions that we do not have the ability to show in detailed, realistic art.

Stuff-It Looks Different From Here:

❑ **Reproducible 5A, p. 43**

❑ pens or pencils

❑ paper

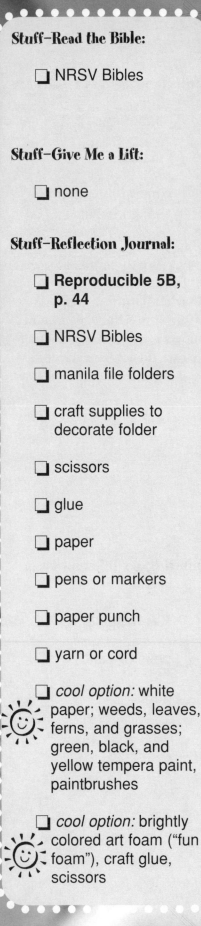

Stuff–Read the Bible:

☐ NRSV Bibles

Stuff–Give Me a Lift:

☐ none

Stuff–Reflection Journal:

☐ **Reproducible 5B, p. 44**

☐ NRSV Bibles

☐ manila file folders

☐ craft supplies to decorate folder

☐ scissors

☐ glue

☐ paper

☐ pens or markers

☐ paper punch

☐ yarn or cord

☐ *cool option:* white paper; weeds, leaves, ferns, and grasses; green, black, and yellow tempera paint, paintbrushes

☐ *cool option:* brightly colored art foam ("fun foam"), craft glue, scissors

Read the Bible Time: 10 minutes

Ask for three volunteers to read Psalm 130:1, 5; John 14:27; and John 19:25-27. Have them read their Scripture passages one at a time, asking the following questions in between.

• Psalm 130:1, 5. **What is the psalmist asking God to do?** (to hear him) **What does the psalmist hope for?** (the word of the Lord)

• John 14:27. **What is Jesus saying he gives us?** (peace) **What does Jesus tell us not to do?** (be worried or afraid)

• John 19:25b-27. **What is happening?** (Jesus is about to die and he asks John to take his mother into John's home and care for her as if she is John's mother.) **Because John and Mary both loved Jesus, what do you think they will do for each other?** (comfort one another)

Give Me a Lift   Time: 5 minutes

Divide tweens into pairs. Be certain each pair has a similar body size and weight.

Say: Sometimes when we experience an exit or feel a loss, it helps to have someone give you a lift. Just knowing someone understands helps us feel better. Let's play a game giving each other a real lift!

Have the pairs sit on the floor facing one another. With feet flat on the floor and toes touching, they are to reach forward and grab hands. Then by pulling together, they try to come to a standing position. Once that is accomplished, have them try to sit back down using the procedure in reverse.

Cool Option: Have tweens try this in groups of three or more.

DEPART

Reflection Journal Time: 10 minutes

Make covers for a reflection journal. Give each tween a manila file folder (old, used ones are okay). Have various craft supplies where everyone can share them. Invite the tweens to cut the folders and trim them to make a cover for their journals.

Give each tween several photocopies of the journal page (**Reproducible 5B, p. 44**). Have them punch holes through the pages and covers so they can tie them together with yarn or cord.

Say: **When we experience an exit or a loss, we have many emotions. One way to deal with those emotions is to give them to God. You can use your journal to help you share your experience with God. The Bible reassures us and helps us have strength when we need it. Choose one or two Bible verses that might help you.** You might suggest they add Psalm 23 and the Lord's Prayer (Matthew 6:9-13) on a blank journal page.

Ten Christian Commitments Time: 5-8 minutes

Pass out photocopies of "Ten Christian Commitments" (**Reproducible 3B, p. 28**). Have a volunteer read the first commitment.

 Teacher Tip: Reproducible 3B will be used again next week. There will be a different question to ask as a result of that day's subject.

Ask: **Can any of you give an example of how this applies when we are experiencing an exit in our lives?** Ask volunteers to read each commitment and ask for examples of each.

Together repeat the "Affirmation of Us."

Pray: **Dear God, thank you for being with me when things are hard. Thank you for giving me the strength to get through it. Thank you for the people in my life who I can trust when I need to talk. Thank you for the comfort I have been given. Help me to help others when they are in pain. Help me to have the compassion to share their pain and the ability to comfort them. Amen.**

PLAN PLUS

Spinning Out of Control Time: 10 minutes

Say: **Sometimes we have hard things happen in our lives. Someone leaves or dies and we feel a loss. Sometimes it is hard to imagine what our life will be like without them. Let's make something that will remind us that when our life feels like it is spinning out of control, we know God is with us and we can get through it.**

☀ Cool Journal Cover Options:

• Make jungle prints using white paper; a variety of weeds, leaves, ferns, and grasses; and green, black, and yellow tempera paint. Have tweens select and paint their greenery one at a time and lay them paint-side down on white paper. Cover the paper and painted greenery with a second piece of paper. Press down gently and carefully remove the top sheet and each piece of greenery. When paint is dry, use painted sheet as front cover of the journal.

• Have tweens cut brightly colored art foam ("fun foam") just a little larger than the reproducible. Cut smaller shapes from various colors to glue onto the front of their journals.

Stuff—Ten Christian Commitments:

❑ **Reproducible 3B, p. 28**

❑ **"Affirmation of Us" poster, p. 64**

❑ masking tape or pushpins

Stuff—Spinning Out of Control:

❑ salad spinner

❑ six-inch paper plates

❑ three bright colors of tempera paint

❑ paper towels

Stuff—Encourage One Another Game:

❑ paper

❑ safety pins

❑ pens or pencils

Stuff—Pray for Each Other:

❑ candles

❑ drip protectors

❑ matches

❑ *optional:* penlights

Teacher Tip: Check the fire regulations in your area to know if lit candles are allowed in your classroom. If not, use penlights. As explained in the activity, give one penlight to the first tween. Have that tween hand the penlight to the person for whom he or she prayed. Then give the first person a penlight to keep. Continue replacing the penlights as tweens pass them on, until each tween has one.

Have a salad spinner, six-inch paper plates, and three bright colors of tempera paint. One at a time, have each tween place a paper plate in the bottom of the salad spinner and pour small amounts of three colors of paint in different areas of the plate. Put the top on the spinner and have the tween spin it for a few seconds. Remove the painting and let dry. You will need to rinse the spinner immediately when the last plate is done.

Encourage One Another Game Time: 10-15 minutes

Give each tween a piece of paper and have someone pin it on his or her back. Ask the tweens to circulate and write one thing they like about each person on that person's piece of paper. Be sure that each tween signs everyone else's paper.

Allow time for tweens to read for themselves what others have written.

Say: It feels good to be encouraged. When we experience an exit or a loss, we need encouragement even more. We can help others who are experiencing something hard and help them get through it.

If you know your group well, you might wish to allow time for each tween to read his or her paper to the group. If a tween is shy, he or she may prefer for you to read it or for it not to be read at all. If you choose this option, know your group well—tweens are not always kind to each other when things like this are being read.

Pray for Each Other Time: 10-15 minutes

Darken the room enough so that lit candles can be seen. Have everyone sit in a circle. Give each tween a candle that has a drip protector. Light one candle. Ask the tween holding that candle to pray aloud or silently for another member of the class who is present in the circle. After completing the prayer, have that tween go over to the person he or she just prayed for and light his or her candle, and then return to his or her seat with the candle still lit. Have the tween whose candle was just lit pray for another person in the circle and then light his or her candle. Repeat the process until everyone has been prayed for and everyone has a lit candle. As teacher, you should participate in this prayer circle.

Make sure all of the candles are extinguished at the end of the activity.

Reproducible 5A

It Looks Different From Here

Sally has been told by her mother that her father is very, very sick. Sally has always taken her problems to her dad, but now she is unsure that he can help her since he feels so bad. What can Sally do?
- **a.** Go to her father and ask how she might be able to help him.
- **b.** Talk to her mother to see if it is okay to still talk to her father about her problems.
- **c.** Go to her friends and ask them how they might handle this delicate situation.
- **d.** Visit her favorite aunt for advice.
- **e.** Talk to her pastor since he has been visiting her father routinely.

Tim has seen his parents argue almost every night. Lately, the conversation has turned toward a divorce. Tim knows that if his parents break up, his parents may each move to a different town. Tim feels helpless and fears if he doesn't do something on his own he will lose one of his parents forever. What can he do?
- **a.** Try to talk with both of his parents about his fears.
- **b.** Side with one or the other parent to help that parent deal with what is going on.
- **c.** Run away in hopes that it will draw his parents back together.
- **d.** Stay out of it and hope for the best.
- **e.** Let his parents' best friends know about what is going on.

Tanya has noticed that her mother is spending less time at home because her grandmother is living in the nursing home. Tanya realizes it is placing a strain on the rest of the family because her mom is gone so much. Dad says things that hurt her mother, but Tanya understands why he says them since she feels the same way. What can she do to prevent further deterioration of her family?
- **a.** Tell her mother that her dad is saying hurtful things because she is gone so much.
- **b.** Talk to her mom about getting her sisters and brothers to help out some.
- **c.** Give up her allowance in hope that her mother can get someone else to help out.
- **d.** Encourage her dad to talk with her mom to find an answer.
- **e.** Go to her friends to see what they might say about it.

Michael has just learned that his older brother is about to be deployed for military service. His mom is very sad about it and cries a lot. Michael is also sad since he is close to his brother. Dad won't talk about it. He just stays quiet. What should Michael do?
- **a.** Comfort his mother and talk with her about it.
- **b.** Ask his dad to understand his mom's sadness and to talk with her.
- **c.** Talk to his brother about it.
- **d.** Ask the pastor to visit and help his family through this difficult time.
- **e.** Focus on his own feelings and decide he can't do anything for anyone else.

© 2005 Abingdon Press. Permission is granted for the original purchaser to reproduce this page for use in the local church or educational setting. Copyright notice must be included on all reproductions.

Journal Page

When I am sad: "The LORD is near to the brokenhearted, and saves the crushed in spirit." (Psalm 34:18)

When I am afraid: "God is our refuge and strength, a very present help in trouble." (Psalm 46:1)

When I am angry: "A soft answer turns away wrath, but a harsh word stirs up anger." (Proverbs 15:1)

When I am worried: "Cast all your anxiety on him, because he cares for you." (1 Peter 5:7)

When I am depressed: "Those who wait for the LORD shall renew their strength, they shall mount up with wings like eagles, they shall run and not be weary, they shall walk and not faint." (Isaiah 40:31)

When things have worked out okay: "I will give thanks to the LORD with my whole heart; I will tell of all your wonderful deeds." (Psalm 9:1)

Date:

What happened:

How I feel:

What I need:

A Scripture that helps:

My prayer:

© 2005 Abingdon Press. Permission is granted for the original purchaser to reproduce this page for use in the local church or educational setting. Copyright notice must be included on all reproductions.

THE POINT

Our faith serves as an anchor while the seas of change surge within us and around our families.

THE SKILLS

Tweens will
• learn to accept change as an inevitable part of life.
• develop coping skills.
• learn about owning all feelings.

THE BIBLE

Luke 2:41-52; Ecclesiastes 3:1-8

THE PLAN

PREPARE yourself

Change is a part of life. Any change, whether it is difficult or welcomed, may be a source of stress for tweens. Tweens want to appear cool, knowledgeable, and experienced. In reality, they do not yet have all the coping mechanisms needed to work through many of the changes that life presents.

Look for warning signals that your tweens are not coping. If you see behavior problems, angry outbursts, withdrawal from the group, physical problems unusual for that child, or depression,

PREPARE your session

Stuff to collect:
- ❏ NRSV Bibles
- ❏ paper
- ❏ pens or pencils
- ❏ watch or timer
- ❏ adult clothes, hats, purses and briefcases
- ❏ two laundry baskets
- ❏ old newspapers
- ❏ masking tape
- ❏ small bag
- ❏ scissors
- ❏ masking tape or pushpins
- ❏ instant camera and film
- ❏ glue
- ❏ heavy paper
- ❏ watercolor paint and paintbrushes
- ❏ postcards
- ❏ *optional:* envelopes and stamps
- ❏ **Reproducible 6A, p. 51**
- ❏ **Reproducible 6B, p. 52**
- ❏ **Reproducible 3B, p. 28**
- ❏ **"Affirmation of Us" poster, p. 64**

Stuff to do:
1. Make photocopies of Reproducibles 6A, 6B, and 3B.

2. Cut Reproducible 6B into strips and put in a bag (see "Change Litany" activity).

you may need to talk with the tween's parents. Professional help may be needed.

Parents and other adults are still the most influential factor in a tween's life. As a tween's life changes their family life will also change. Their ability to communicate openly and freely without judgment is key to acquiring the life skills that get us through the tough changes. As their teacher, you can model acceptance, patience, and willingness to listen.

Help your tweens see the relevance of Bible stories to their own lives. **Luke 2:41-52** is about Jesus when he was a tween. Help your tweens understand that Jesus was not being defiant, but he was fulfilling what God planned him to be.

Ecclesiastes 3:1-8 assures us that all life has a cycle and an order, whether we understand it or not. If your tweens wonder, "Why did someone I love have to die? Did God plan that?" help them understand that we don't know why things happen. Our faith helps us know that in the world things change; God is there for us through all of it and our faith will sustain us throughout life changes.

GATHER

Change Is the Game Time: 8 minutes

Divide the tweens into teams of three or four. Give each team a piece of paper and a pen or pencil.

Say: Work in your groups to list as many things as you can that change and how they change. (For example, a caterpillar becomes a butterfly.) You have two minutes. Do not let the other teams see or hear any of the words you discover. Let's see which team can list the most changes.

Have the teams count the number of items they have listed. Let one team read their list and then the other teams read those items that they had that were different.

Say: Everyone has changes in their lives. We will all experience more changes in our lifetime than we imagine. Some changes we will expect and be prepared for. Others we won't expect and we will have to figure out how to deal with them. Our faith in God can be our anchor to help us hold on when a change feels overwhelming.

Stuff–Change Is the Game:

☐ paper

☐ pens or pencils

☐ watch or timer

Change Relay Time: 10 minutes

Say: Not all changes are bad. Some changes we look forward to and are fun. Let's have fun playing a change relay.

Divide the class into two teams. Have each team stand in line on one end of the room. On the other end of the room, have two piles containing equal numbers of large adult male and female clothes, hats, purses, and briefcases. Beside each pile place an empty laundry basket.

Say: When I say "Go," the first player on each team has to run to the pile in front of their team, select one item from the pile and put it on, then run back to the team, take off the item, and give it to the next player on the team. That player must put on the item, run to the laundry basket, take off the item and place it in the laundry basket, select a new item, put it on, run back to the team, take it off, and give it to the next team member to put on. Let's see which team can get everything into the laundry basket first.

Change Check Time: 5-10 minutes

Pass out "Check It" (**Reproducible 6A, p. 51**). Ask them to check the changes they have experienced in the last year and mark if the change was good, bad, or just okay.

INTERACT

Read the Bible Time: 10 minutes

Say: We all experience change—that's normal. Even Jesus experienced change when he was your age.

Ask for volunteers to read Luke 2:41-52.

Ask: What change did Jesus experience? (His priorities changed from childish things to serious learning in the Temple.) How do you think Joseph and Mary felt when they could not find Jesus? How do you think they felt when they found Jesus? What do you think they might have said to him when they were alone? Do you think Jesus deliberately disobeyed his parents? Why do you think Jesus decided to stay at the Temple? (Jesus was beginning to mature in his understanding of his life's mission. He probably didn't think about what was happening outside of the Temple.)

Change Is Not a Choice

Stuff-Change Relay:

❑ adult clothes, hats, purses, and briefcases

❑ two laundry baskets

Teacher Tip: If you do not have space for a relay, you may wish to substitute the "Change Faces" activity in Plan Plus for this activity.

Stuff-Change Check:

❑ **Reproducible 6A, p. 51**

❑ pens or pencils

Stuff-Read the Bible:

❑ NRSV Bibles

Say: Jesus did not defy his parents. The indications are he got caught up in God's Word and didn't really think about his parents worrying about him. In all other accounts in the Bible Jesus was never thoughtless of another person's needs. Like Jesus, you are at an age when your life is changing. Your attitudes are changing. You are beginning to think about what you want to do about college and careers. All of these changes are normal. They are part of God's plan.

Change Storm   Time: 5-10 minutes

Say: Sometimes change comes so unexpectedly that we feel like we are in the middle of a storm and have nothing to hold on to. Let's play a game to see how it feels to be in a change storm.

Ask everyone to rip pieces of old newspaper and loosely wad them into as many balls as possible. Explain that each ball represents a change we might experience in our lives.

Divide into two teams of even numbers (you may have to play). Use masking tape to mark two parallel lines four- or five-feet apart. Have Team A stand inside the lines on the floor. Have Team B divide so that they can stand on the outside of both lines. Have the newspaper balls separated and placed where the players on Team B can reach them easily.

Say: When I say "Go," Team B should grab the newspaper balls and start throwing them inside the lines. Team A will toss them back out and try to keep the storm of newspaper balls away.

Stop them after three minutes. Count the number of newspaper balls inside the lines. Begin play again, this time with Team B inside the lines and Team A throwing the newspaper balls.

Say: Change can be hard and even overwhelming, but we can't stop it, no matter how hard we work. The Bible assures us that change is part of God's plan.

Read the Bible   Time: 5-10 minutes

Ask volunteers to read Ecclesiastes 3:1-8. **Ask: How are the times given in these verses?** (As opposites; "A time to be born, and a time to die.") **What do you think this means?** (Change is inevitable and natural.) **Say: When change occurs, we can feel confident that God is still in control. Our faith is our anchor in a storm of change.**

Stuff-Change Storm:

❑ old newspapers

❑ masking tape

Stuff-Read the Bible:

❑ NRSV Bibles

Talk! Talk! Talk! Time: 5 minutes

Have tweens sit in a circle and do an "add on" story. The first person says one line to the story and the next person adds one sentence to the original one. This continues until everyone has added a message. Ask them to make the message about a tween who is experiencing a change. Let's see what the story becomes.

After the story, **Ask: What was the change? Was it a good or a bad change? Why? How different is the story than when it first began**?

Say: This game of talking was fun. But when we are going through changes, especially tough changes, it is very important for us to talk. When you are experiencing a change, you can talk with your parents. If for some reason you can't talk to your parents, talk to another adult who you trust. You can talk with a relative, neighbor, teacher, counselor, or pastor. Just remember—talk about the changes you are going through. You do not have to go through them alone.

Change Litany Time: 5-8 minutes

Photocopy and cut apart the strips for Ecclesiastes 3:1-8 (**Reproducible 6B, p. 52**) and put them in a bag. Ask each tween to draw a strip from the bag. Have everyone walk around the room saying the words on their strips until they find the person with the opposite strip. Then ask them to try to figure out what order they should be in. When done have them read their strips aloud in order. Have someone check the Bible to see if they are correct. Read it again. After each pair says their part, everyone is to say together, **We praise you, God.**

DEPART

Ten Christian Commitments Time: 5-8 minutes

Pass out photocopies of "Ten Christian Commitments" (**Reproducible 3B, p. 28**). Have a volunteer read the first commitment.

Ask: Can any of you give an example of how this applies when we are experiencing a change in our lives? Ask volunteers to read each additional commitment and ask for examples of each.

Change Is Not a Choice

Stuff–Talk! Talk! Talk!:

❑ none

Stuff–Change Litany:

❑ **Reproducible 6B, p. 52**

❑ NRSV Bibles

❑ small bag

❑ scissors

Teacher Tip: If you have a small class, have the tweens take turns drawing strips. Have them put the strips in order and each tween take a turn reading one of the strips. As each set is read, have everyone say together, **We praise you, God.**

Stuff–Ten Christian Commitments:

❑ **Reproducible 3B, p. 28**

❑ **"Affirmation of Us" poster, p. 64**

❑ masking tape or pushpins

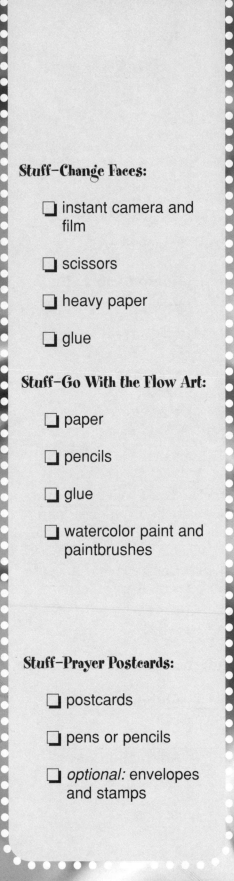

Stuff–Change Faces:

❏ instant camera and film

❏ scissors

❏ heavy paper

❏ glue

Stuff–Go With the Flow Art:

❏ paper

❏ pencils

❏ glue

❏ watercolor paint and paintbrushes

Stuff–Prayer Postcards:

❏ postcards

❏ pens or pencils

❏ *optional:* envelopes and stamps

Together repeat the "Affirmation of Us." **Pray: Dear God, you have given us so much. Please help us with the changes we will have in our lives. Help us each day to grow in wisdom and strength as Jesus did. We trust you, God, to be with us. We know you have planned the time for all things. Help us to help others. Thank you, God. Amen.**

PLAN PLUS

Change Faces Time: 10 minutes

Take a photo of each tween's face using an instant camera. Make sure each tween is the same distance from the camera and that everyone is looking straight ahead. Cut each photo into four pieces. Have tweens work together to put together new faces using pieces from four different photos. Have them mount the changed face onto heavy paper. Hang the photos on the wall.

Go With the Flow Art Time: 5 minutes

Use this activity at the beginning and end of class. **Say: Change is something that will happen many times in our lifetime. Sometimes change is hard, and we have to hold on to our faith to get through it. Sometimes change is good and makes us happy. Sometimes change is just okay and we can go with the flow.**

Have tweens use a pencil to draw a faint flowing design on paper, then squeeze a thin line of glue over their pencil lines. Suggest they use the glue quickly to make sure the design flows. Let the glue dry until the end of class. Have them paint watercolors inside the glue lines on their pages. Encourage experimentation with colors.

Prayer Postcards Time: 5 minutes

Say: We can help others and give them comfort when they are experiencing difficult changes. One way we can give them support is by praying for them.

Hand out postcards to the tweens. Ask each tween to think of a person he or she knows who is experiencing a difficult change. Encourage each tween to write a prayer and a personal note for that person on a postcard. Have tweens deliver the postcards in person or if they need to be mailed, have stamps and envelopes available for mailing them.

Reproducible 6A
Check It

Event	Good	Bad	Just Okay
hair got longer			
got hair cut			
gained weight			
lost weight			
got a new friend			
lost a friend			
started at a different school			
moved into a different house			
got a new pet			
lost a pet			
started a new hobby			
got a new brother or sister			
parents divorced			
parent started a new job			
go to a different church			
family member died			
changed size of clothes I wear			
changed the kind of music I like			
parents have a new car or truck			

© 2005 Abingdon Press. Permission is granted for the original purchaser to reproduce this page for use in the local church or educational setting. Copyright notice must be included on all reproductions.

Reproducible 6B

Ecclesiastes 3:1-8

For everything there is a season, and a time for every matter under heaven:

a time to be born	a time to embrace
a time to die	a time to refrain from embracing
a time to plant	
a time to pluck up what is planted	a time to seek
	a time to lose
a time to kill	a time to keep
a time to heal	a time to throw away
a time to break down	a time to tear
a time to build up	a time to sew
a time to weep	a time to keep silence
a time to laugh	a time to speak
a time to mourn	a time to love
a time to dance	a time to hate
a time to throw away stones	a time for war
a time to gather stones together	a time for peace

© 2005 Abingdon Press. Permission is granted for the original purchaser to reproduce this page for use in the local church or educational setting. Copyright notice must be included on all reproductions.

Live It! My Family

TWEENS AND PARENTS TOGETHER

THE POINT

Our faith grows and our families strengthen when tweens, parents, and God engage in dialogue.

THE SKILLS

Tweens and parents will
• understand the family's need for obedience to a higher truth.
• explore situations from one another's perspective.
• learn new techniques for initiating conversation.

THE BIBLE

Isaiah 1:18-20; Luke 2:52

THE PLAN

PREPARE yourself

To prepare yourself for working with tweens and parents together, read carefully "Parent and Tween Communication" on page 61. Also read carefully today's Scriptures.

• **Luke 2:52**—This verse says "Jesus increased in wisdom and in years, and in divine and human favor." Human favor would indicate a maturing relationship with other persons—presumably including his parents. For relationships to mature, all parties need to work at communication. Given the familial faux pax that had taken place

PREPARE your session

Stuff to collect:
❑ NRSV Bibles
❑ construction paper
❑ markers
❑ masking tape
❑ *optional:* Bible-times costumes
❑ scissors
❑ basket
❑ deep red crepe-paper streamers
❑ large sheet of paper and marker, chalkboard and chalk, or markerboard and erasable marker
❑ chairs
❑ stapler and staples
❑ covered dishes for potluck supper (provided by families)
❑ disposable plates, napkins, cups, and utensils
❑ *The United Methodist Hymnal* or another music resource
❑ **"Affirmation of Us" poster, p. 64**
❑ **Reproducible 2B, p. 20**
❑ **Reproducible 7A, p. 58**
❑ **Reproducible 7B, p. 59**

For ☀ *cool options:*
❑ rhythm instruments

Stuff to do:
1. Make photocopies of Reproducibles 7A and 7B.
2. Cut out Table Blessing cards **(Reproducible 7B, p. 59)**. Cut on solid lines, fold on dotted lines. Overlap tabs A and B. Staple or tape together for base of cards.
3. Cut crepe paper into sections and roll up (two per person) (see "Let Us Argue It Out" activity).

Stuff–Tag Them Acrostically:

❏ construction paper

❏ markers

❏ masking tape

Example:

Son of Rex and Delores Brown
A grandson of Robert and Agnes
  Graham
Middle school student
Unappreciated younger brother of
  Stephanie Brown
Excellent trombonist
Little brother of Thomas Brown

Cool Option: If you are meeting at a time other than Sunday morning and have more time, continue this activity. After creating the acrostic with their first names, the participants will circulate among the group and have other persons (a different one for each letter) use the letters in their last names to continue the acrostic.

Stuff–Present "One Rebellious…":

❏ **Reproducible 2B, p. 20**

❏ *optional:* Bible-times costumes

❏ *cool options:* rhythm instruments

Cool Option: To present the story in rap style, have some of the tweens provide accompaniment either with rhythm instruments or with body music—hand claps, finger snaps, leg pats, and so forth.

in Jerusalem just prior to this verse—Mary and Joseph losing track of their son and Jesus failing to make sure his parents knew where he was, it's obvious that even the Holy Family had some work to do in the area of communication.

• **Isaiah 1:18** says, "Come now, let us argue it out, says the LORD." The CEV is a bit more delicate: "I, the LORD, invite you to come and talk it over." "'Come now, let us reason together,' says the LORD" is how the verse is translated in the NIV. Jerusalem is on trial, already standing convicted of sins "like scarlet." The arguing or reasoning is not geared at determining guilt or innocence, but at strengthening a relationship—based on obedience—between the people and their God. In our communications as families, we find ourselves living in obedience to the One who calls us into a growing relationship with God and with one another.

GATHER

Tag Them Acrostically Time: 15-20 minutes

Greet participants as they arrive and have each person make a nametag on construction paper. Have them write their first names vertically on the paper, and then create an acrostic using the letters in their first names. The horizontal words will describe them—especially their connections to family members.

Gather the participants together and have family members introduce one another using the acrostics.

Present "One Rebellious Father, Two Rebellious Sons" Time: 5 minutes

Have the tweens present the story of the prodigal son for the parents (**Reproducible 2B, top of p. 20**). Choose persons to portray the characters in pantomime. Use biblical costumes if available. Let others read the story in parts. Introduce the story as follows.

Say: Jesus told the story of a lost son who was later found. We tend to think that this son is the only rebellious one in the story, but he has company. The older son—the one who stays home and is obedient to his father—rebels when his younger brother is welcomed back with no questions asked. But the father is also somewhat rebellious. The laws were clear on how rebellious sons were to be treated, but the father chooses to overlook the law and do what came naturally to him—to love his sons no matter what.

INTERACT

Parent and Tween Flip-Flop Time: 15-25 minutes

Make a photocopy of the "Parent and Tween Flip-Flop Cards" **(Reproducibles 7A & 7B, bottom of pp. 58-59)**, cut them apart, and place them in a basket. Have one or more sets of parents and tweens come forward, select a card, read it to the group, and then roleplay the situation, with the parents taking the roles of tweens, and the tweens taking the roles of parents. Do as many of the roleplays as time permits.

Ask: How did you feel about the role you were playing? Were the parents believable as tweens? Were the tweens believable as parents? How might any of the situations been handled differently and more effectively?

Let Us Argue It Out Time: 10-15 minutes

Have the group stand in a large circle. Give each one a photocopy of "Based on Isaiah 1:18-20" **(Reproducible 7B, top of p. 59)** and a red crepe-paper streamer. Indicate where the streamers are to be thrown. Everyone will start moving to the left, kind of like wrestlers dancing around one another, and read the litany on the reproducible.

Say: This passage is not about figuring out if anyone is guilty of sin. That has already been determined. The argument or debate is about what we are to do next, once we recognize that we have all been involved in sinful behaviors—things that have separated us from God and from other persons.

Have everyone be seated. **Ask: Imagine an argument—perhaps a real argument. You may or may not be involved, but you are present. How does your head respond to the argument? How does your back respond to argument? How does your stomach respond to the argument? How do your arms respond to the argument? How do your legs respond to the argument?**

Divide the participants into five small groups and assign a body part to each small group. Give them a couple of minutes to discuss how their body part responds, and then report to the whole group.

Ask: Have we resolved an argument when one person forces the other to submit to what he or she thinks is right? Rather than one person submitting to the other, perhaps the more

Stuff—Parent and Tween Flip-Flop:

☐ **Reproducible 7A & 7B, pp. 58-59**

☐ scissors

☐ basket

Stuff—Let Us Argue It Out:

☐ **Reproducible 7B, p. 59**

☐ scissors

☐ deep red crepe-paper streamers

☐ large sheet of paper and marker, chalkboard and chalk, or markerboard and erasable marker

Stuff—Conversation Circles:

☐ chairs

Conversation Circles Questions
1. If you needed to be someplace bright, where would you go in your house?
2. If you were to compare yourself to a character on TV, who would it be and why?
3. If you were to compare your parent(s) to TV characters, who would they be and why?
4. The quietest my family has ever been was when…
5. What is the room in your house where God might be most welcome and why?
6. What is one way in which your parents parented that you would like to parent too?
7. If you could place an order for someone to add to your family, what would you write on the order form?
8. What is your favorite family story and why?
9. How would your family be different if God were not a part of it?
10. What are three changes that have taken place in your family in the past year and how do you feel about them?

Stuff—Depart:

☐ "Affirmation of Us" poster, p. 64

☐ NRSV Bibles

effective approach is to start out with ground rules for the argument to which everyone agrees to be obedient. **What might some basic ground rules be for discussing something parents and tweens disagree about?** As the participants offer ground rules, record their ideas on a large sheet of paper, a chalkboard, or a markerboard. Have each person vote for the three ground rules that he or she believes to be the most important. Add up the votes, and underline those that receive the most votes.

Conversation Circles Time: 20-25 minutes

Have tweens arrange their chairs in small circles of four to seven persons. They will be sitting with their backs to the center of the circles. The parents will then position themselves in front of their son or daughter. Even where only one parent is present, two chairs should be placed in front of each tween. If more than one tween is present from a family and only one parent, have a parent from another family or another adult present sit with the extra tween.

Once tweens and parents are in place, have the tweens rotate one position to the left in their circles so that they are now sitting across from a parent(s) other than their own. Select questions or sentence completions from the list in the margin for the tweens and parents to discuss. Every two or three questions, have the tweens rotate again and talk with another parent or set of parents. Continue until they are back with their own parents, and use the last three questions for this pairing.

DEPART Time: 5 minutes

Invite a tween to read Luke 2:52 aloud. **Say: This verse both admits that Jesus had some growing up to do and celebrates that he did it. He was better able to respond in appropriate ways to what was going on around him as he got older, and his relationships matured—with God and with other persons, which would most likely have included his parents. Jesus had a kind of rocky start at becoming what we consider a teenager, but in his day would have been considered becoming an adult. However, he continued to grow, continued to mature, and the Bible tells us both he and his relationships grew stronger in the process.**

Pray: In silence, pray for the members of your family who are here. (pause) **Pray for the tweens who are present.** (pause) **Pray for the adults who are present.** (pause) **Teach us, O God,**

a new appreciation for what it means to be a tween, for what it means to be the family of a tween, and for you. These things we ask in Jesus' name. Amen.

Lead the group in repeating the "Affirmation of Us."

PLAN PLUS

Enjoy a Meal Together Time: 20-35 minutes

Each family should bring a covered dish to contribute to the dinner. Use disposable tableware and divide up responsibility for setting tables, arranging the food, preparing beverages, and clean up so that all participants have tasks to do and no one is prevented from taking part in the session.

Place the Table Blessing Cards (**Reproducible 7A, top of p. 58**) so that they can be shared. Make photocopies of the cards. Cut on solid lines and fold on the dotted lines. Overlap Flaps A and B and staple or tape them together to form the base.

Invite everyone to stand and join hands. Lead the table blessing either by speaking it together or singing it to the tune of "For the Beauty of the Earth" (*The United Methodist Hymnal*, No. 92).

Signals Time: 10 minutes

Extra time? Have parents and tween work on some hand/body signals that they could use to alert the other of feelings without having to come up with the words to express themselves.

1. You're embarrassing me.
2. You don't want to go there.
3. I really don't know what to say.
4. Is this your best offer?
5. I'm feeling trapped.
6. I don't agree but I don't want to embarrass my (your) friend.
7. What can I do to help?
8. Not now, but maybe later.
9. That hurt me.
10. I think you're great but don't want to make a big deal out of it right now.

Stuff—Enjoy a Meal Together:

❏ **Reproducible 7A, p. 58**

❏ covered dishes for potluck supper (provided by families)

❏ disposable plates, napkins, cups, and utensils

❏ scissors

❏ stapler and staples

❏ *optional: The United Methodist Hymnal* or another resource with the music for the hymn "For the Beauty of the Earth"

Stuff—Signals:

❏ none

TABLE BLESSING

At this table, God, we stand
side by side and hand in hand;
grateful for the food prepared,
for the time in which it's shared;
for your blessings, day and night;
loved ones to our left and right.

Bring to mind the folks in need,
whom we're called to love and feed.
Grant us calm and joy and skill,
strengthen us to do your will,
set us free from guilt and shame;
this we ask in Jesus' name.

FLAP A

TABLE BLESSING

At this table, God, we stand
side by side and hand in hand;
grateful for the food prepared,
for the time in which it's shared;
for your blessings, day and night;
loved ones to our left and right.

Bring to mind the folks in need,
whom we're called to love and feed.
Grant us calm and joy and skill,
strengthen us to do your will,
set us free from guilt and shame;
this we ask in Jesus' name.

FLAP A

TABLE BLESSING

At this table, God, we stand
side by side and hand in hand;
grateful for the food prepared,
for the time in which it's shared;
for your blessings, day and night;
loved ones to our left and right.

Bring to mind the folks in need,
whom we're called to love and feed.
Grant us calm and joy and skill,
strengthen us to do your will,
set us free from guilt and shame;
this we ask in Jesus' name.

FLAP B

TABLE BLESSING

At this table, God, we stand
side by side and hand in hand;
grateful for the food prepared,
for the time in which it's shared;
for your blessings, day and night;
loved ones to our left and right.

Bring to mind the folks in need,
whom we're called to love and feed.
Grant us calm and joy and skill,
strengthen us to do your will,
set us free from guilt and shame;
this we ask in Jesus' name.

FLAP B

Parent and Tween Flip-Flop CARDS

Plan a one-day family outing within fifty miles of home.

Friends from out of state are coming for a visit with their four kids and dog and will be staying with you. Decide where everyone will sleep.

Your family has just received an unexpected inheritance of $13,000. How will you spend it?

The local Christmas store's going-out-of-business sale begins tomorrow. Plan your outdoor display in order to take best advantage of the sale.

You are going to add on to the house. What kind of space do you need the most?

© 2005 Abingdon Press. Permission is granted for the original purchaser to reproduce this page for use in the local church or educational setting. Copyright notice must be included on all reproductions.

Live It! My Family

Based on Isaiah 1:18-20

All: Come now, let us argue it out, says the LORD.

Parents: Let's talk about it rationally.

Tweens: Let's have ourselves a debate.

Parents: Let's dialogue together.

Tweens: Let's listen to both sides.

Parents: Let's have a civil conversation.

Tweens: Let's be reasonable.

Parents: Let's get this thing resolved.

Tweens: Let's get on with it

All: Let's argue it out!

Parents: Though your sins are like scarlet (*toss streamer*),

All: they shall be like snow;

Tweens: though they are red like crimson (*toss streamer*),

All: they shall become like wool.

Parents: If you are willing and obedient, you shall eat the good of the land . . .

All: for the mouth of the LORD has spoken.

Put together a plan for evacuating your house in the event of a fire.

Your family has been asked to coordinate a response to the microburst that destroyed the home of a family whose kids have been bullying the kids in your family for the past three years.

An older sibling has joined a religious cult while away at college and is coming home for a weekend—the first time in four months.

Mom has had an excellent job offer out of state and wants the family to help her decide what to do.

Your grandfather has died unexpectedly and as a family you are planning his memorial service.

© 2005 Abingdon Press. Permission is granted for the original purchaser to reproduce this page for use in the local church or educational setting. Copyright notice must be included on all reproductions.

More Cool Stuff

MOVIE OPTIONS

Freaky Friday—Choose a clip from this movie to start a discussion about looking at things from the other person's point of view.

Cheaper By the Dozen—Could use a clip from this movie to start a discussion about siblings.

Be sure to preview all video clips to avoid any content that would be objectionable in your setting.

CAUTION: Your church must have an Umbrella License® from the Motion Picture Licensing Corporation to show any portion of a film in any setting other than home use. Check with your church office to see if your church has this license before using this activity. For more information see the Motion Picture Licensing Corporation web site at www.mplc.com.

PARENTS AND TWEENS TOGETHER

Freaky Friday Roleplays—For "Tweens and Parents Together" you might wish to show a clip from the movie. Make "P" and "K" nametags (as was done in the "Bottom Skootch" activity in Lesson 2). Divide into teams. Have each team come up with a situation and then roleplay with the parents acting as tweens and the tweens acting as parents (wearing the appropriate nametags).

CDs—Have your tweens bring their favorite CDs and their parents to bring their favorite CDs. Play short snippets of each of the CDs. Talk about why they are their favorites.

CHOOSE A SERVICE PROJECT

Contact a local agency that does work with foster children. See what needs they have that your group might be able to provide. Sometimes they need things as simple as bags to transport their few belongings when they get moved from one home to another.

Another option is to adopt a grandparent in the church—someone who has no grandchildren or whose grandchildren live far away. Go to visit, send cards, and/or weed his or her garden. Talk about the experience.

Parent and Tween Communication

Parents and tweens really want to communicate. Many of them just haven't figured out how to get the conversation started or how to keep it going. What's the hang-up? Fear—pure and simple.

Fear of what? Some fears are different for parents and tweens, and others are the same. Let's consider a few possibilities.

Sometimes parents fear
• being rejected by their tweens
• having the truth about their own youthful indiscretions exposed
• feeling inadequate—not having the answers
• saying the wrong thing and prompting a strong emotional response
• remembering and re-experiencing the pains of their own middle school years

Sometimes tweens fear
• being ridiculed or not taken seriously
• starting to express feelings and not being able to stop
• revealing their ignorance
• upsetting parents or having parents dwell on whatever the tween has mentioned
• triggering parental surveillance or punishment

Sometimes tweens and parents both fear
• sitting in silence
• risking embarrassment
• being overwhelmed by the task
• having little in common
• talking about faith issues

Directed conversation seems to be one of the best ways to get communication started. **Why does it work?**

• Especially when parents have had limited experience, given their own parents' discomfort with dialogue, this offers something, which is better than nothing.
• Parents and kids are not alone but surrounded with others who are making their own stumbling attempts at dialogue.
• Someone else is directing the process, which takes the pressure off of the parents. They just have to follow the directions.
• Some people tend to try a little harder when they're in public.
• This setting has the feel of a practice session rather than a prime time performance, also reducing the pressure placed on both parents and tweens.

For Parents:
Letting Go While Holding On

Having a tween is a pretty tall order. Sometimes they act like they are twenty-five years old and you are proud as you can be; the next moment they are acting like they are three years old and someone has taken their favorite toy.

They want to grow up and be independent. They want to become a person separate from you. They push the boundaries and try your patience. At the same time deep down they want to know exactly where those limits are (that's why they spend time pushing them), and they want to know that no matter what you will love them and hold on to them.

Hormones are racing. Body parts are growing at different rates (larger ears, hands, feet, and so forth while perhaps height hasn't caught up).

They are thrown into a completely different school environment just about the time that they have learned to handle the old environment well. Homework increases, and choices increase—including drugs, sex, cigarettes, and cheating in school.

And of course, in the middle of this, you as a parent have become "uncool" and down right dumb. Communication with a tween at this stage often takes one of two forms. Confrontational—when you talk it's a battle. Or non-informational—that's when a tween tells you exactly what you want to hear; why no one they've ever known has ever been offered a drink or drugs; they don't even know what sex is. (In the very unlikely event that that's true at the moment, it won't be by the time they have entered seventh grade.) Some parents do manage to keep very open communications with their tweens throughout their formative years, but it's not easy.

Tweens make some pretty bad choices. In fact, the brain predisposes them towards poor choice-making. The frontal lobe where judgment resides is not fully developed until the early to mid-twenties. At this stage there is very little activity in the frontal lobe because their brain is using a lot of energy with growing and hormones. When a preteen (or a youth) makes good choices they often come from a lifetime of good habits and good parental modeling. When they make bad choices— sometimes they have just have been overcome with pressure, with literally not using their brains, or the desire for instant gratification comes over them.

What can you do?

• Pray for the patience and understanding needed to raise a tween.

• Be there. Day after day, problem after problem.

• Be assured that eventually they will grow up—you will have gray hair and will have lost a lot of sleep, but they will grow up.

• Communicate. Talk with your tween—not at them—and LISTEN, really listen to what they have to say.

• Set reasonable boundaries. Now is not the time to become a "friend." It's the time, more than ever, to be a parent, but also time to let go of some things that are appropriate for the age.

• Be an example. How you live you daily life affects tweens much more than anything you can say.

© 2005 Abingdon Press. Permission is granted for the original purchaser to reproduce this page for use in the local church or educational setting. Copyright notice must be included on all reproductions.

Faith Friends Program

A Faith Friend is an older person who mentors a tween in the faith and who can be called upon in times of a "faith emergency." A Faith Friends program can be developed and used in different ways.

Formal Program

You might wish to have a formal mentoring program where you carefully pair up each tween with a specific Faith Friend and these Faith Friends come to the first and last tween sessions of your *My Family* sessions (not the Tweens and Parents Together session—that would be counterproductive). Faith Friends could do the activities along with your tweens.

Caution: If this approach is used be sure that you have ways to ensure that the tweens get to do most of the talking and/or work.

If you use this as a formal mentoring program, have your Faith Friends call or e-mail your tweens at least once a week.

Semi-Formal Program

You might wish to choose another group that meets at the same time and have them come to the first and sixth sessions of your *My Family* sessions. Depending upon the number of tweens, Faith Friends might be assigned one or more tweens or tweens might be assigned one or more Faith Friends. (Young adult or older adult classes work best for mentoring this age group.)

Tweens choose from the available adults who will be the person they would call on if they have questions of faith or just want to talk about what's happened at school

Caution: Educate your adult class beforehand. They must agree to be willing to talk with a tween if called or e-mailed.

Informal Program

Let the tween choose somebody in the church that they feel comfortable with to be a person that he or she would choose to call or e-mail if they feel they need a Faith Friend to talk with.

• No matter which type of Faith Friend program you use, hand out a Faith Friends Emergency Card to each tween and to each mentor and let them exchange phone numbers and e-mail addresses.

• **CAUTION:** DO NOT ENCOURAGE TWEENS AND FAITH FRIENDS TO MEET ALONE AT ANY TIME.

• **IMPORTANT:** PARENTAL PERMISSION MUST BE OBTAINED FOR ANY INVOLVEMENT IN THE FAITH FRIENDS PROGRAM.

Affirmation of Us

I am a child of God.

I know God created me.

I am worthwhile.

I am valuable as I am.